Katherine Bebo

111 Places in Poole That You Shouldn't Miss

Photographs by Oliver Smith

emons:

For Mum and Dad.
Thanks for bringing me up in such an amazing place.

© Photographs by Oliver Smith, except:
J. Stock Photography (ch. 13, 18, 30, 39, 50, 59, 81, 85, 87, 101, 103)
Waveslider Photography (ch. 54)
Jake Moore (ch. 2)
Artist Credits: Band featured in chapter 85 is The Paul Booth Quartet.
© Cover motif: shutterstock.com/tinkivinki
Edited by Alison Lester
Layout: Eva Kraskes, based on a design
by Lübbeke | Naumann | Thoben
Maps: altancicek.design, www.altancicek.de
Basic cartographical information from Openstreetmap,
© OpenStreetMap-Mitwirkende, ODbL
Printing and binding: Grafisches Centrum Cuno, Calbe
Printed in Germany 2021
ISBN 978-3-7408-0598-2
Revised second edition, April 2021

Did you enjoy this guidebook? Would you like to see more?
Join us in uncovering new places around the world on:
www.111places.com

Foreword

As I was hovering high above the sea, suspended by an aquatic fly-board, I couldn't help but think, 'Isn't Poole wonderful?' I had the same thought as I sipped locally made sparkling wine in a vineyard. And again as I wandered around the former garden of a literary legend. In fact, I thought, 'Isn't Poole wonderful?' 111 times throughout the process of researching and writing this book. When I began, I imagined that I'd struggle to find 111 things in Poole that would be worthy to include – places that were not only interesting but also little-known and somewhat quirky. Boy, was I wrong! The places I discovered could have filled two books. Some spots I had previously passed thousands of times without giving a second glance – too busy, too preoccupied. But writing *111 Places in Poole* opened my eyes. Now when I see something that looks like it might have a story attached – a statue, a plaque, a wonky tree – I vow to Google it when I get home. Perhaps this book will inspire the same curiosity in you.

Technically, a lot of the entries aren't in Poole per se. My rule of thumb when I was researching was that everything should be, more or less, within a 30-minute drive of Poole. I didn't venture to Bournemouth as that could be an entire book in itself. I've done my darndest to make sure that I have all my facts straight, but if I have included any errors please accept my apologies. Note that in the 'Getting There' sections, for places in the Isle of Purbeck and Wareham, I have given driving instructions, but you may choose to take the chain ferry to Studland, then find your way from there.

Some of the places I've written about are well-known – Poole Park, Durdle Door, Old Harry Rocks – but I've sneaked past the obvious to discover something surprising. Whether you're a visitor to Poole or a seasoned local who thinks you know *everything* about your hometown, my hope is that this book will not only make you smile, but also leave you raising your eyebrows and saying, 'Well, I never…'

111 Places

1 A. R. Wallace's Grave

The evolution of one-upmanship

Ever heard of Antonio Meucci, Howard Florey or Sir Humphry Davy? Probably not. But all of them made world-altering discoveries (the telephone, penicillin and the lightbulb, respectively) for which someone else got the glory. You can add Alfred Russel Wallace to this list of people who had their thunder stolen. He arrived at the theory of natural selection independently of Charles Darwin. In 1858, he sent an article to Darwin, his friend and fellow biologist, detailing his theory. It was later published, along with Darwin's own ideas. This motivated Darwin to publish *On the Origin of Species*, which received international interest. The duo compared notes on a number of other topics, including sexual selection and warning colouration among species. Wallace dedicated *The Malay Archipelago*, one of the 19th century's most popular books of scientific exploration, to Darwin. They were as thick as thieves, yet Darwin had the limelight while Wallace skulked on the sidelines (perhaps he liked it that way, preferring to stay at home and categorise the 80,000 beetles he acquired in the archipelago).

Wallace moved to Poole in 1888, settling first in Parkstone and then Broadstone. Here he built his house, Old Orchard, which was located on what is now Wallace Drive. He died at home on 7 November, 1913, at the ripe old age of 90 – that's survival of the fittest right there. It was suggested that he be buried at Westminster Abbey alongside Charles Darwin, but it was his wish to be laid to rest at Broadstone Cemetery.

His grave is marked by the, shall we say, 'unusually shaped' seven-foot trunk of a 146-million-year-old fossilised tree. Wallace is said to have collected it himself from Portland in Dorset. Was he aware how phallic it is? Perhaps he's looking down from heaven thinking, 'I may have been overlooked in life, but at least I get to be the big man in death.'

Address Broadstone Cemetery, 83 Dunyeats Road, Broadstone BH18 8AF | Getting there Bus 4 towards Wimborne Minster to Broadstone Middle School | Hours Daily 9am–4pm | Tip Broadstone Library, on the aptly named Story Lane, houses a plaque celebrating the life and discoveries of Alfred Russel Wallace.

2 Aquatic Jetpacks
To infinity and beyond!

Ever fancied yourself as a superhero? If so, strapping on a flyboard and zooming up to 33 feet in the air may be the closest you'll come to fulfilling your dream. Poole has long been a popular spot for watersports – waterskiing, wakeboarding, windsurfing, kayaking, kitesurfing and, now, flyboarding. It involves trusting your feet to a pair of boots that are attached to a board with jet nozzles underneath. The board is connected by a long hose to a jet ski, which powers the board and propels the thrill-seeker/superhero wannabe into the air. It is Fun with a capital F.

Aquatic Jetpacks is the first company in the UK to offer coastal flyboard experiences. It operates out of The Watersports Academy, and takes flyboarders out into the open sea from Sandbanks Beach. Old Harry (ch. 60) is in the background, waiting to laugh at the silly faces you pull when you excitedly realise you're flying, or when you make a spectacular face-plant into the water. To maximise your time in the air, the knack is to keep your body straight, your head up and to adjust the weight on your feet slightly forwards and backwards to keep your balance, similar to how you would on a Segway. The session lasts around 25 minutes; any longer and your thighs may never forgive you.

In 2017, Aquatic Jetpacks coordinated The Grand Splash-ional, a PR stunt for the bookie Coral to highlight its involvement with The Grand National. Ross Ceaton, who owns Aquatic Jetpacks, was one of the six 'jockeys' who took to the water with a flyboard and model of a horse's head to 'race' through Liverpool Watersports Centre. The event received much media attention, featuring in *The Times*, *The Daily Express*, *The Sun* and *The Daily Mirror*.

Flyboarding is an experience like no other. Zooming high above the ocean, you'll feel like Superman, Thor and the Silver Surfer have nothing on you: Captain Jetpack. Shazam!

Address The Watersports Academy, 15 Banks Road, Sandbanks BH13 7PS, +44 (0)1202 706784, www.aquaticjetpacks.com, info@aquaticjetpacks.com | **Getting there** Bus Breezer 60 towards Sandbanks to Shore Road | **Hours** Certain Fridays and Sundays Apr–Oct (check website for details) | **Tip** Jetski Safaris is Aquatic Jetpacks' sister company and offers jet ski tours and powerboat trips (www.jetskisafaris.co.uk). Hold on to your hat!

3 __ Assyrian Frieze
Candy cash

At school, what was the most expensive thing at your tuck shop? A bag of penny sweets? A can of fizzy pop? A chewy bar you'd be picking out of your teeth all through maths? Until 1994, the students at Canford School had no idea that their tuck shop – or 'grubber' as it was known – was a goldmine. A 3,000-year-old frieze, hanging near a dartboard, was discovered to be an antiquity (rather than the worthless plaster cast copy it was believed to be) and was sold for £7.7 million during an auction at Christie's London that was over in a three-minute bidding frenzy – with the price increasing in increments of £100,000. *Going, going... gone!*

The five-foot-high treasure was excavated from the lost city of Nimrud in the Nineveh region of Assyria (now Iraq) by archaeologist Sir Austen Henry Layard between 1845 and 1851. It had once decorated the walls of King Ashurnasirpal II's palace, where he lived during his 883 – 859 BC reign. Many of Layard's finds went to the British Museum but this frieze was part of a set gifted to Lady Charlotte Guest – Layard's first cousin – because she paid for and published his book about his first trip when no one else would. As thank-you presents go, this one sure beats a box of Cadbury's Roses. Guest lived at Canford Manor, which became Canford School in 1923. All of the friezes in the set, bar this one, were sold, with many believing it had gone missing – perhaps to the bottom of the Tigris River.

The unexpected windfall from the sale of the frieze was used to pay for scholarships and bursaries, a girls' boarding house, a new sports centre and a theatre. Fittingly, the latter is named the Layard Theatre, and the foyer houses this replica of the upper half of the original frieze. There is another replica in the tuck shop, now called the Nineveh Café. A grand memento that reminds students of the sweetest deal ever to go down at their school.

Address Layard Theatre, Canford Magna, Wimborne BH21 3AD, +44 (0)1202 841254, www.canford.com, office@canford.com | **Getting there** By car, A350, A349, A341 to Canford Magna | **Hours** Viewing by arrangement; contact the Layard Theatre staff via email | **Tip** The sports centre and theatre funded by the sale of the frieze are open to the public, as are Canford's golf club and tennis courts (if you join as a member).

4   Aunt Mimi's Plot

A legend's house reimagined

John Lennon referred to Sandbanks as 'the most beautiful place I know'. This is probably why he bought a bungalow for his Aunt Mimi there in 1965. Called Harbour's Edge and located at 126 Panorama Road, the six-bedroom, waterside property set the Beatle back £25,000, at a time when the average cost of a house was around £3,500. The same day as Mimi's funeral – held at Poole Crematorium and attended by Yoko Ono – her home was put up for sale. It was later demolished and a new house built. The property on the plot now has been renamed 'Imagine' and was on the market in 2018 for £7.25 million.

Mimi bought her nephew his first guitar, telling him: 'The guitar's all right as a hobby, John, but you'll never make a living out of it.' John later had these words set into a plaque, which was hung on a wall at Harbour's Edge – as were his gold discs. Oh, the irony! When he wanted to escape Beatlemania, Lennon would seek refuge at his aunt's abode, where he would relax on the balcony overlooking the harbour or turn cartwheels on the beach. He also enjoyed sailing along the River Frome to Wareham in a small boat belonging to Mimi's neighbour. Could this be the inspiration of the first line of 'Lucy in the Sky with Diamonds': 'Picture yourself in a boat on a river'?

Panorama Road – dubbed 'Millionaires' Row' – is said to be one of the most desirable streets in the world. With just 13 houses on the strip – each with a panorama of Poole Harbour – it's the most expensive stretch of coastal real estate, with a combined property value of £93 million. The road's 'price per square foot' exceeds that of waterfront streets in Monte Carlo and Miami. In the 1920s, local developer Thomas Kingsbury was offered land in Sandbanks for £5 an acre. He declined, reasoning that you can't build on sand. This same land is now worth £20 million an acre. Hindsight is a wonderful thing. And so are the views.

Address 126 Panorama Road, Sandbanks BH13 7RB | **Getting there** Bus 12 towards Sandbanks or Breezer 50 towards Swanage to Ferry Approach | **Tip** If you want a meal with a view, visit the Rick Stein restaurant just around the corner (www.rickstein.com/eat-with-us/rick-stein-sandbanks).

5_ Barford Ice Cream
Get the scoop

Farmers are a hardy bunch. Being reliant on the land, animals and the whims of Mother Nature, they have to be. They roll with the punches and do what they've got to do. Which is what Wendy and Chris Pope did in 2006 when they found that the abysmal price they were getting for their cows' milk was proving detrimental to their livelihood.

Enter Barford Farmhouse Ice Cream. Using the milk produced from their herd of 250 Holstein-Friesians, they invested in a unique machine that cooks a batch of ice cream at the top, then freezes it on the bottom after a handle is turned and the mixture has fallen through to this section. While this batch is freezing, another one can be cooking on the top. Multitasking to the max. This homemade process allows very little air into the ice cream, which means it's solid and it's creamy. *Mmm!* It's not a large-scale operation, and that's just how the Popes – and their customers – like it. When they first set up shop, the goal was to take their milk from 'cow to cone' (which is the name of their limited company) in under an hour. They have since sold their cows, and now get their milk from a young lad milking his herd in Sturminster Marshall just a mile away.

Very much a family affair, the Pope's daughter-in-law, Jo, makes all the ice cream. Of the 18 flavours, two are always sorbets and one is a special that changes frequently – it could be anything from tiramisu to white chocolate, lemon curd to rhubarb-and-ginger sorbet. Barford is experimental with its flavours and has been known to whip up cracked black pepper ice cream, basil ice cream and beetroot sorbet. Diabetics are also catered for, as are those needing a gluten-free cone. But you won't just be dolloped a scoop and sent on your way; there's a quaint garden, complete with fishpond, blooming flowers and various nooks and crannies where you can sit and savour your delectable treat.

Address Barford Farm, Cowgrove Road, Wimborne BH21 4BY, +44 (0)1258 857969, www.barford-icecream.co.uk, enquiries@barford-icecream.co.uk | Getting there By car, A350 to Sturminster Marshall, then take High Street and Mill Lane | Hours 11.30am – 5.30pm (weather permitting), Apr – June Wed – Sun & bank holidays, July – Aug Tue – Sun & bank holidays. Check website for Sept update | Tip Take a tub of yum home with you in either a 0.5-litre or 1-litre container.

6 Benjamin Jesty's Grave
A bovine breakthrough

In 1986, Roald Dahl wrote an open letter urging parents to vaccinate their children. He described how his daughter had died from measles in 1962, before a reliable measles vaccination had been discovered. This heart-wrenching plea resurfaced in recent years in response to many parents refusing to immunise their kids. The subject of vaccinations and the controversy surrounding them is nothing new. Benjamin Jesty – the farmer who performed the first ever vaccination for smallpox – knew this only too well. While Edward Jenner is widely acknowledged as the man who eradicated the deadly smallpox, it was actually Jesty who administered the vaccine first, as his gravestone states.

Jesty lived with his wife, Elizabeth, and three small children, along with two milkmaids – Ann Notley and Mary Reade – at Upbury Farm in Yetminster, Dorset. In 1774, smallpox had raged through the village, but Ann and Mary had nursed their sick relatives without becoming infected themselves. Milkmaids rarely caught smallpox because most of them, when young, had caught cowpox (a disease similar to smallpox), meaning they were immune. This got Jesty thinking. Having asked Elizabeth for her hand four years previously, he now asked for her arm – a much less romantic proposition but one that most likely saved her life. He located some infected cows and, using a stocking needle, transferred the cowpox disease into his wife's scratched arm, and then repeated the procedure on his two- and three-year-old sons. It was a success: Elizabeth and the boys never contracted smallpox. Which makes Jesty the first vaccinator, 22 years ahead of Jenner.

Jesty is buried alongside Elizabeth in the Worth Matravers churchyard. His pioneering inoculation was a bold, risky move, but one that paid off. Had he not tried it, the date of death on his wife's gravestone could easily have been many decades earlier.

Address St Nicholas of Myra Church, Worth Matravers, Swanage BH19 3LQ | Getting there By car, A350, A35, A351, B3069, turn right and drive through Worth Matravers, the church is on the right. Jesty's grave is in the churchyard, near the cluster of trees closest to the church. | Tip For a more detailed account of Jesty's story, read *The First Vaccinator*, written by the inhabitant of next door's Lobster Cottage, on sale inside the church.

7 Bermuda Triangle Bar

Beware you don't get lost

When is a bookcase not a bookcase? When it's a secret door that leads to a cool bar. Find the hidden button on the 'bookcase' inside The Bermuda Triangle pub and the door will magically open, inviting you to venture up the stairs and into a world that serves 20 different gins, 14 different whiskeys, 12 different rums and 7 different tequilas. Order yourself a cocktail (how does a 'Bossmopolitan' or a 'Phil Collins AKA The Easy Lover' grab you?), then sink into one of the plush velvet or leather sofas and, heck, you may find you never want to leave.

Decked out to give an edgy-yet-cosy gentlemen's club vibe – think exposed brick, faux dead-animal rugs, a wood burner with piled up logs, and a warthog's head on the wall (it's fake… hakuna matata!) – it's actually proved more popular with women than men since it opened in 2017. This is in direct contrast to the pub downstairs (established in 1870) which, very often, is a veritable sausage fest. Serving 16 different draught beers and hosting frequent live-music nights, it runs with the Bermuda Triangle theme and is bedecked with framed newspaper cuttings documenting various aircraft and ships that have inexplicably been swallowed by this mysterious stretch of ocean, as well as nautical bits and pieces, maps, and an old newspaper article about Miss Bermuda 1939, who is the grandmother of one of the regulars.

Much like the boats and planes that the Bermuda Triangle has claimed, certain objects inside the pub go missing, too. These, however, pop up again in a different location. Indeed, the staff keep themselves amused by relocating the following things: a *Star Wars* Stormtrooper, an Action Man, a parrot, a red bus and a black rat. When you visit, see if you can locate them… then see if you can locate the secret button on the bookcase. Need a hint? Well, let's just say that the name of his school rhymes with 'Pogwarts'.

Address 10 Parr Street, Parkstone BH14 0JY, +44 (0)1202 748087,
www.bermudatrianglepub.com, info@bermudatrianglepub.com | Getting there Bus 1
towards Purewell or M1 towards Castlepoint, to Ashley Cross | Hours Upstairs bar:
Wed–Sun 7pm–midnight | Tip If you're in the mood to play dress-up, don one of
the 12 different hats hung up by the bar, take a selfie and then post it to The Bermuda
Triangle Facebook page.

8__ Blandford Fashion Museum
Would you like dyes with that?

Whether it's flicking through the pages of *Vogue*, critiquing an A-lister's dress on the red carpet or blanching at Lady Gaga's 2010 meat get-up, for many people, fashion is fabulous, fun and fascinating. If you agree, you should visit the Blandford Fashion Museum. Set up in 1996 by Betty Penny MBE, it originally housed her own collection (known as the Cavalcade of Costume) but this has since trebled in size to around 5,000 items due to donations from fellow fashionistas. Most pieces have a story to tell, and some date back to as far as 1740. There are 13 display areas over two floors, with the exhibitions being swapped every year or so on a rolling programme. Displays could be anything from underwear through the ages (including 'open drawers' to allow a woman to spend a penny more easily) to styles that changed the fashion world (such as Coco Chanel's 'flapper' look and Mary Quant's miniskirt) to ladies of Dorset (including famous sculptor Dame Elisabeth Frink, who had a penchant for Blandford-made jackets).

The museum has an ongoing arrangement with world-famous fashion designer Bruce Oldfield, whereby he loans it one of his pieces for a period of time, then replaces it with another. Known as the man who dressed Princess Diana in the 1980s (in 1985, she wore a Bruce Oldfield black velvet gown for a portrait by photographer Lord Snowdon, which later fetched £50,000 at a charity auction), he has also showcased his fancy frocks on Diana Ross, Joan Collins, Faye Dunaway, Barbara Streisand, Jerry Hall, Sienna Miller, Taylor Swift, Rihanna and Catherine Zeta-Jones. Oh, and Camilla, Duchess of Cornwall (#awks). In 2008, he turned his haute couture hand to designing the McDonald's uniform. Hesitant to take on the commission at first, he then reasoned that if Pierre Cardin could design the uniforms of the Paris road sweepers then he could earn his McFashion stars.

Address Lime Tree House, The Plocks, Blandford Forum DT11 7AA, +44 (0)1258 453006, www.blandfordfashionmuseum.co.uk, info@blandfordfashionmuseum.co.uk | **Getting there** By car, A350, Bournemouth Road, West Street to The Plocks. On-street parking opposite the museum, short-stay car park on Church Lane. | **Hours** Mon, Thu – Sat 10am – 4.30pm, closed end Nov – Feb | **Tip** Don't miss the displays on Dorset's glove-making, button-making and lacemaking (in 1698 there were 500 lacemakers in Blandford, and it was considered some of the finest lace in England).

9 Branksome Viaducts

An arch enemy struck

All of the mighty Branksome Viaducts are still standing, but if the Luftwaffe German air force of 1941 had had better aim, they wouldn't be.

On 27 March, a lone German bomber – believed to be targeting the two railway viaducts in Bourne Valley – hit the canteen of the adjacent gasworks, during lunchtime. People dived under tables for cover, but two bombs killed 33 people (6 were teenagers, the youngest being 14) and injured 23 more. It was Poole's worst air raid and the largest single loss of life in the town during World War II. As the pilot of the Messerschmitt Bf 110 aircraft flew over the drill hall on Alder Road and approached the viaducts, he showered machine gun fire down, the damage of which can be seen today on the viaduct in Surrey Road. A third bomb was dropped but landed in between the railway tracks of the Branksome Triangle and didn't explode. Stories later emerged of how fate had spared some of the gasworkers – one leaving five minutes earlier for a haircut, one popping out for a cigarette and another who should've been in the canteen but had forgotten his sandwiches.

One of the railway lines running over the viaducts served the Royal Navy Cordite Factory at Holton Heath, loading up trains with the ammunition it manufactured there. A few days before the gasworks was obliterated, the Germans had tried and failed to bomb the cordite factory. Presumably, Plan B – destroying the viaducts and their vital transport links – was then implemented.

The impressive viaducts were built in the 1880s, using materials from the local brickworks located where Sainsbury's on Alder Road now stands. Four times a day, workers would transport bundles of 400 bricks to the site. During construction, a horse and cart carrying bricks fell into the then-hollow structure and couldn't be rescued, so had to be covered with infill. Bleak times all round.

Address Branksome BH12 1HQ | Getting there Bus M1 towards Castlepoint, M2 towards Southbourne to Branksome Tesco or 16 towards Bournemouth to Yarmouth Court | Tip A bronze 'Roll of Honour' plaque inside St Aldhelm's Church in Branksome commemorates those who died at the gasworks on 27 March, 1941.

10_Briantspuddle Dairy
Milking it

The next time you're in Debenhams, perhaps enjoying a cup of tea in the cafe, take a moment to think about Ernest Debenham as you're pouring the milk. The grandson of William Debenham, who founded the department store, Ernest was a pioneer in the dairy and agriculture industries, as well as the chairman of Debenhams (busy guy). In 1914, he bought a number of farms around the village of Briantspuddle, which became part of the 10,000-acre Bladen Estate.

Briantspuddle was home to one of the most forward-thinking agricultural businesses of its time, with Debenham embarking on a 'farming experiment' which aimed to 'cut out the middle man'. Many aspects of farming were developed at Briantspuddle but it was the dairy that was perhaps the most innovative. Known as 'The Ring' due to its arrangement of buildings in a semi-circular shape, the dairy was the hub for collecting, testing and packaging milk from the farms around the estate.

Debenham strived for the highest standards of milk production, with a laboratory constantly testing milk for bacteria. Bonuses were offered to workers from farms supplying milk with the lowest bacterial count. In the 1920s, around 1,000 gallons of milk were processed a day; this figure grew to 10,000 gallons a day for people to drink, and 10,000 gallons to be used in cheese and butter. That's a lotta cows!

The Ring was the first dairy to have large-scale milking machines in Dorset. Steam generators produced electricity, with the exhaust steam being used to pasteurise the milk. This was highly cutting-edge stuff, as was the use of paper cartons (50 years ahead of Tetra Pak), which were lighter to transport and kept the milk fresher for longer. Now, the dairy has been converted into various private homes. Like the rest of the village, they are thoroughly charming, and it's no doubt that the residents feel like the cat that got the cream.

Address Dorchester DT2 7HT | **Getting there** By car, A350 and A35 to Dorchester Road, then the exit towards Briantspuddle. Drive through the village until you see a stone directing you to The Old Dairy. | **Tip** The village's *Madonna and Child* war memorial was created by Eric Gill, who also produced the controversial *Prospero and Ariel* statue standing at the entrance to the BBC's Broadcasting House in London.

11 Broad Stones

What live streaming used to look like

Ever wonder how places get their names? Well, when it comes to Broadstone, a suburb of Poole that over 10,000 people call home, wonder no more! In 1840, three 'broad stones' were laid across the Blackwater Stream, near Brookdale Farm, so that people could cross the water without getting their feet wet. (Brookdale Farm was probably the second building to be constructed in the area, after the nearby Albion Inn.)

These are two of the original stones, located outside the Broadstone United Reformed Church. The stone-laying across the stream was the kind deed of Mr Horwood, who lived at Brookdale Farm. Perhaps the whiff of soggy, smelly socks wafting onto his property got too much for him to bear.

When the railway was built in 1872, Blackwater Stream was forced underground into a large culvert and the original stones were preserved at the instigation of the resident of the house on the corner of The Broadway and Ridgeway. He arranged to have 'Broadstone' carved onto what was believed to be the middle stone, so that people would know when they had arrived here. He placed it near his home but, unfortunately, it was stolen decades ago. A replica (minus the 'Broadstone' carving) now sits in the same spot, outside The Blackwater Stream pub – previously called The Stepping Stones in honour of these rocks. Find it by the pavement, next to the Ridgeway road sign.

Around 1800, prior to Broadstone acquiring its current name, it was recorded on the map as 'West Heath'. This old name lives on today in Westheath Road. In 2017, a study found Broadstone to be the third most desirable place to live in the UK (pipped to the post by Norwich, and Bebington in the Wirral), taking into consideration factors like work-life balance, local schools and green spaces. With its village vibe, cute shops and interesting history, locals agree it's a positively rockin' place to live.

Address Broadstone United Reformed Church, 1 Higher Blandford Road, Broadstone
BH18 9AB | Getting there Bus 3 towards Wimborne Minster to United Reformed Church,
or bus 18 towards Broadstone to The Broadway | Tip The Blackwater Stream pub's walls are
adorned with much information about Poole's past. Pop in for a history lesson and a pint.

THIS TABLET COMMEMORATES
150 YEARS OF THE FOUNDING
OF THIS CHURCH FELLOWSHIP
1847 - 1997
AND WAS UNVEILED BY
Dr. D. M. THOMPSON
MODERATOR OF
THE GENERAL ASSEMBLY
U.R.C.
9th FEBRUARY 1997

12 Broadstone Tapestry
A stitch in time

Inside the Broadstone Methodist Church hangs this fine-wool tapestry, made in 1990 to mark the 100th anniversary of the church. Each of the eight scenes, embroidered by members of the parish, depict something relating to Broadstone's history.

Moving clockwise: in the top left, there's the farm with a 'broad stone' in front of it – a reminder of how Broadstone got its name (ch. 11). Next to that is Sharland's Brickworks, which has since been knocked down; Broadstone Recreation Ground on Charborough Road now stands in its place. Brickmaking was the first industry in the area other than farming and, in the 1800s, Elias Sharland built many of the brick houses, churches and schools in Broadstone. Below is the Broadstone railway station. Opened in 1872, it was then called New Poole Junction but the name was later changed, before it eventually closed in 1969. Today, The Junction Sports & Leisure Centre takes its place. Under that sits Alfred Russel Wallace, the famous Broadstone resident who played a pivotal role in developing the theory of natural selection, for which Charles Darwin got the glory (ch. 1).

The bottom right display is of the 1920 war memorial standing proud at Broadstone Recreation Ground. Left of that is Broadstone First School, followed by an everyday scene from the 1890s, outside French's store, which was a one-stop shop for anything and everything. A vintage Home Bargains, one might say. Finally, the Lavender Farm. In the early 1900s, fields of lavender were grown to be made into perfumes, lavender bags and 'perfume bricks' (used to scent clothes in drawers) at the Dorset Lavender Factory. This factory burned down in 1935 and the farm was demolished in the 1960s, but much lavender remains in the area today. Lavender Way and Lavender Lodge are a nod to the area's flowery history.

Forget life's rich tapestry; visit Broadstone's rich tapestry.

Address Broadstone Methodist Church, Lower Blandford Road, Broadstone BH18 8DT, +44 (0)1202 600696, www.broadstonemethodist.org.uk | Getting there Bus 4 towards Oakley or Wimborne Minster, to The Broadway | Tip Don't miss the colourful mural outside the church stating: 'Each of us is a single note, together we make a masterpiece!'

13 Chain Ferry Cross

A unique ferry crossing

'My chains fell off – my heart was free, I rose, went forth, and followed Thee.' These lyrics, taken from the hymn 'And Can It Be That I Should Gain?' by Charles Wesley (just one of his 6,000 hymns) can be found in Lady Saint Mary Church in Wareham. Alongside them is this cross constructed from part of the old Studland ferry's chain. Set in Purbeck stone, it was put here in 1991 to indicate the start of the Decade of Evangelism – a call to Christians to 'promote' Christ during the closing years of the millennium.

The ferry began operating in 1926, using its underwater chains to pull cars and foot passengers across the harbour from Sandbanks to Studland and back again. Its car capacity has increased 220 per cent since then, from 15 to 48, and now over 1.25 million cars use the vessel every year.

The current ferry, which was introduced in 1994 and is 242 feet long, is the fourth to operate this service, but the first to have a name – *Bramble Bush Bay*. The third ferry has now been converted into a floating base for an oyster farming operation in Poole Harbour, located near the north shore of Brownsea Island.

The chain ferry has certainly seen some drama over the years. There have been rescues of people who have been dragged under the ferry by the current, and collisions with boats that have been unable to fight against the tide. The chains have broken a few times, too – one time resulting in the tense evacuation of passengers into a lifeboat. There's even been a stand-off between police and a traveller with a horse and wagon, when he was refused entry onto the ferry because his nag wasn't in a horsebox.

The ferry has an excellent safety record, however, and your journey will most likely occur without incident. If you're nervous, though, as you embark, think of the chain ferry cross in Lady Saint Mary Church and ask a fellow passenger to wish you 'godspeed'.

Address Lady Saint Mary Church, 18 Church Street, Wareham BH20 4ND, +44 (0)1929 550905, www.warehamchurches.org.uk, parish.office@warehamchurches. org.uk | **Getting there** By car, take A3049, A35 and A351 to St John's Hill in Wareham; bus Breezer 40 to South Bridge | **Tip** The church font, dating from about 1100, is unique, being the only hexagonal lead font in existence.

14__Chococo

Cocoa bean, cocoa gone

Do you think that scones with clotted cream and jam is the ultimate in delicious? Guess you haven't tried Chococo's chocolate chip scones served warm with clotted cream and dulce de leche caramel? If the thought of this gets your sweet tooth a-tingling, you'd better get down to this luxury 'chocolate house' in Swanage tout de suite. If the offerings of brownies, carrot cake, chocolate fondue, millionaire's shortbread, gelato, biscuit cake, flapjacks, and all other manner of tempting treats sound a little 'tout de sweet' for you, they also cater for those seeking something savoury – think soups, toasties and scones with flavours such as sundried tomato and feta, goat cheese and pesto, and cheese and Marmite.

Chococo, opened in 2002, is one of the first UK artisan chocolatiers. It has both a cafe and a shop, and offers chocolate tastings, workshops and parties. It's won 85 national and international awards and prides itself on producing high-quality, handmade chocolate goodies. Some of what they create is sophisticated; some is a bit of fun, like the chocolate teapot, which is about as useful as a... oh. They also sell boxes of chocolates where the box is made out of chocolate. The. Box. Is. Made. Out. Of. Chocolate.

Chococo works with 'Raisetrade' chocolate, whereby the cocoa beans are made into chocolate at the country of origin – like Madagascar, Venezuela, Vietnam, Colombia and Grenada – so that the local economy is supported.

In collaboration with Lush (ch. 51), who adapted their orangutan soap mould for a chocolate version, Chococo has also created Tuan and Tuantoo – cute, melt-in-your-mouth orangutans. With every sale, money is donated to the Sumatran Orangutan Society (SOS) to help rebuild the rainforest and protect orangutans' habitat, which is under threat due to the huge expansion of palm oil plantations. Deliciously ethical.

Address 21C-23A Commercial Road, Swanage BH19 1DF, +44 (0)1929 422748, www.chococo.co.uk, info@chococo.co.uk | **Getting there** By car, A350, A35 and A351 to Rempstone Road in Swanage, continue onto Station Road, turn right onto Commercial Road; bus Breezer 40 or Breezer 50 towards Studland to Swanage Bus Station | **Hours** Mon–Sat 9.30am–5.30pm, Sun 10am–4.30pm | **Tip** Fancy doing a 'chocolate crawl' around Swanage? Make sure Love Cake on the High Street is another of your scrummy stop-offs (www.lovecakecafe.co.uk).

15 Clavell Tower

Relocation, relocation, relocation

As romantic date spots go, the Tuscan-style Clavell Tower is certainly up there (pun intended). When novelist and poet Thomas Hardy would visit with his first love, Eliza Bright Nicholl (daughter of a Kimmeridge Bay coastguard), in the 1860s, the sweeping views of the Jurassic Coast alone would've been enough for love to bloom. They were also enough for artistic creativity to strike; Hardy drew a picture of a couple walking up the path to Clavell Tower and used it in his *Wessex Poems* book. More recently, the tower inspired P. D. James' 1975 mystery *The Black Tower*. The novel was made into a TV series, using Clavell Tower as the primary location. The tower also featured in the 1985 music video of 'Boy Who Cried Wolf' by Paul Weller's band The Style Council.

In the late 1980s, Clavell Tower was in serious danger of falling into the sea due to erosion. The Kimmeridge cliffs are made of clays and shales that are enough to give Cadbury's Flakes a run for their money in the crumble department – eroding at a rate of about 13 metres a century.

Built in 1830 by Reverend John Richards Clavell, the tower was inching perilously closer to the cliff edge over the years until, in 2005, the task of moving it 25 metres inland began. The Landmark Trust – a charity that rescues and restores historic buildings at risk – took on the project, marking the tower into quadrants and painstakingly dismantling it piece by piece. Each chunk was numbered, inventoried and stored in wooden crates until the time came to put it all back together – a bit like the most elaborate Lego construction ever. Walk up the hill and you can still see the original foundations. Where the tower now stands should be safe for at least 200 years. This gives you enough time to woo the object of your desire up there. It is now fully furnished and sleeps two, so you can stay if you get lucky.

Address Kimmeridge, Wareham BH20 5PF, +44 (0)1628 825925, www.landmarktrust.org.uk, info@landmarktrust.org.uk | **Getting there** By car, A350, A35, A351 and Grange Road to Kimmeridge. Enter the toll road and park by the Wild Seas Centre. Walk down the hill and follow the sign to Chapman's Pool, up the steep steps. | **Tip** Another Dorset Landmark Trust property is Wolveton Gatehouse. Thomas Hardy came here, too, visiting for tea in 1900.

16_Clouds Hill Sleeping Bag
Return of the sack

Thomas Edward Lawrence: archaeologist, army officer, diplomat, scholar, writer, aircraftman and… embroiderer. *Huh?* Yes, as well as all of T. E. Lawrence's achievements – one being his key role in the Arab Revolt, which earned him the nickname Lawrence of Arabia – this capable man also had another skill: needlework. When his neighbour, Henrietta Knowles, made him a pair of sleeping bags, he went to work embroidering *Meum* ('Mine' in Latin) on one, and *Tuum* ('Yours' in Latin) on the other. Both sleeping bags are now back where they belong at Clouds Hill, Lawrence's cottage in the woods, but the 'Tuum' sleeping bag went walkabout for 36 years. It was stolen in 1965, perhaps due to the excitement surrounding the *Lawrence of Arabia* film, which won seven Oscars. In 2001, it was returned to Clouds Hill in a parcel with a Belgium postmark and a note saying, 'This is yours'.

Lawrence entertained some distinguished guests at his modest pad, including playwright George Bernard Shaw, poet Robert Graves, artists Augustus John, William Roberts and Gilbert Spencer, and novelists E. M. Forster and Thomas Hardy (whose own house, Max Gate, is about eight miles away). Many snuggled into 'Tuum' if spending the night. Forster would visit to help Lawrence revise his book *Seven Pillars of Wisdom*, an autobiographical account of the Arab Revolt. The royalties from this were spent on remodelling Clouds Hill, and on his beloved George Brough motorcycles. A keen biker, if Lawrence was around today, he'd no doubt hit Poole Quay for Bike Night during the summer months. *Vroom!*

Sadly, it was one of his greatest pleasures – riding – that led to his demise. On 13 May, 1935, travelling on the road from Bovington Camp, where he was stationed, to Clouds Hill, he had a motorcycle accident. He spent six days unconscious and died on 19 May, aged just 46. Sleep tight, Lawrence.

Address Clouds Hill, King George V Road, Bovington BH20 7NQ, +44 (0)1929 405616, www.nationaltrust.org.uk/clouds-hill, cloudshill@nationaltrust.org.uk | **Getting there** Can be reached via car, train, bike or foot (via the Lawrence Trail) – see website for details | **Hours** Daily 1 Mar – 31 Oct 11am – 5pm | **Tip** There is a Lawrence of Arabia exhibit at The Tank Museum in Bovington (www.tankmuseum.org).

17 Constitution Hill

I spy a stunning view

John Le Carré, author of *Tinker, Tailor, Soldier, Spy*, was born in Poole in 1931. Having been described as 'the world's greatest fictional spymaster' (sorry, Ian Fleming), as a child, he and his brother would play with cap guns at Constitution Hill in Parkstone.

Notorious for shunning publicity and staying out of the limelight, the same can't be said for his family, who were well-known locally. His grandfather was the mayor of Poole, and his uncle spent time as an MP for East Dorset, a deacon at the Parkstone Congregational Church, the chairman of Poole Town FC and, for the 20 years until 1962, a Poole magistrate.

Le Carré's mum, Olive, was living at The Homestead, 22 Penn Hill Avenue, when she met his father, Ronald. They moved into a house on Brownsea View Avenue, which is where Le Carré was born. Little did Olive know that her beau would turn out to be a flashy conman and later be jailed for insurance fraud. She herself was no angel and abandoned her son at the age of five.

It's not only Le Carré (whose real name was David Cornwell) who enjoyed playing at Constitution Hill as a youngster; the same spot holds many happy memories for other Poole locals. Whether it was running down the hill as fast as possible, watching storms roll over Poole, or 'courting' the object of one's desire, it's a special place for many. So special, in fact, that the inscription on one of its benches reads: 'This is where it all started! Married April 1941. In loving memory of Anne and Norman Knight.'

The view over Poole Harbour and beyond is magnificent. A monument points out what you can see in the distance and how far away it is, with Hardy's Monument the farthest at 22 miles. Sitting on a bench, with the beautiful vista in front of you, it's the perfect spot to sit and think. Or sit and read. Word is that John Le Carré's books are worth a gander.

Address Constitution Hill, Parkstone BH14 0QB | Getting there Bus 17 towards Bournemouth to Felton Road | Tip For another gorgeous view of Poole Harbour, head to Evening Hill (BH14 8HR), where many a marriage proposal has occurred.

18 The Courtyard Tea Rooms

How do you like your eggs? Haunted!

Ever eaten eggs inspired by a ghost? Now's your chance! The spinach and mushroom Eggs Annabelle are named after this cosy tea room's resident ghost, who – according to staff – likes to turn lights on and leave bin lids in the middle of the floor. Perhaps she hasn't properly 'passed over' yet because she's reluctant to leave the tempting array of breakfasts, light lunches, homemade cakes and scones on offer. And who can blame her? The tea menu alone – which boasts 24 flavours, many blended in-house, such as the fruity Mango Boost or the smoky Russian Caravan – is enough to elude the afterlife for.

Formally a laundrette, antiques shop and add-on to the neighbouring florist, these quaint tea rooms were also once believed to be a tavern for rum-swilling pirates. They date back to the 16th century, with one wall and most of the flagstone flooring hailing from this era. Tunnels are said to run under the building, used by smugglers to transport their contraband to and from the quay. Such criminal activity is now long gone and the only rebellion you'll find is the encouragement to shirk unnecessary housework – with a sign reading: 'Life is too short to fold fitted sheets'.

With a capacity of just 37, the height of summer often sees queues of eager scone-scoffers and flapjack-fiends snaking around the corner. The awards the establishment has won is testament to the fact that it's worth the wait. A real suntrap, the courtyard comes complete with a fossilised tree stump, climbing plants and winding wisteria. The perfect oasis to tuck into a sandwich named after local sights – who's for a Brownsea or a St James (ch. 89)? Perhaps an excerpt from a poem written by a customer says it best: 'It's tiny but it's cosy; often busy, always friendly… For tea and talk and teacake, the only place to be.'

Annabelle would certainly agree.

Address 48a High Street, BH15 1BT, +44 (0)1202 670358, www.thecourtyardtearooms.co.uk, mail@thecourtyardtearooms.co.uk | **Getting there** 10-minute walk from Poole Bus Station, 4-minute walk from Poole Quay | **Hours** Opening hours vary, see website for details | **Tip** For another tea treasure trove, head to It's Tea at 219 Ashley Road. It stocks more than 350 teas and infusions (www.itstea.co.uk).

19_ The Crown Hotel

Who you gonna call?

If you've ever watched Stanley Kubrick's 1980 film *The Shining*, you'll know there can be something decidedly sinister about twins. Some guests at The Crown Hotel in Poole's Old Town also know this only too well. Born in the 17th century and chained up in the attic by their parents, a pair of deformed twins – who were buried under the floor in the inn's larder after their death – are said to haunt this establishment, freaking people out left, right and centre with their tortured screams.

The Crown is supposedly the most haunted building in Poole with various sightings, hearings and chilling feelings reported over the years. There's been an apparition of a young girl in a white nightdress leaning on a bannister, the sound of horses' hooves, a door rattling violently, another door creaking open with no one on the other side, a gliding blue light melting into a wall, tools being scattered willy-nilly, lights flickering, a closed piano tinkling, objects flying around, the sound of phantom children playing, and 'someone' vanishing into thin air. *Spooky*.

The eerie goings-on here have fascinated ghost hunters from all over the world. They have also fascinated Jane Goldman, the wife of TV and radio star Jonathan Ross. She presented a TV programme called *Jane Goldman Investigates* and visited The Crown Hotel in 2003 to get her supernatural on. (Incidentally, Jane and Jonathan own a 16th-century farmhouse in nearby Swanage.) The current landlady of The Crown was approached by someone wanting to hold a seance in the flat above the pub, which is where she lives with her partner. She politely declined.

If you happen to see a ghost while visiting, don't hang around to see if it'll invite you to play, as the terrifying twins in *The Shining* do. Instead, perhaps head to the bar to steady your nerves with a different kind of spirit. Better make it a double.

Address 23 Market Street, BH15 1NB, +44 (0)1202 672137, www.crownhotelpoole.co.uk, crownhotelpoole@gmail.com | Getting there Five-minute walk from Poole Quay, just by the Guildhall | Hours Mon 3–11pm, Tue–Sun noon–11pm | Tip The Cow pub and restaurant at Ashley Cross is said to be haunted by Molly, an ex-employee of the hotel that once occupied the building.

20 Deans Court Bridge

Sisters are doin' it for themselves

This isn't just a bridge. This is also a one-finger salute to Wimborne's town council. In 1930, the owner of Deans Court, Lady Cordelia Hanham, fell out with the governing body because it tarmacked over Deans Court Lane, the avenue leading to the estate. Outraged, she erected a gate to stop cars from driving up the lane. The council ordered her to remove it, she refused, and the local authority claimed ownership of the lane because – technically – they owned the surface of it. A court case ensued, and Cordelia was forced to get rid of the gate. Furious at the town's ingratitude for her previous contributions (she gave much to the community, including building a rectory for Wimborne Minster), she vowed never to set foot in Wimborne again. But there was a flaw in her plan: the River Allen runs through the grounds of Deans Court and there was no bridge, which meant she had to drive through Wimborne to reach Poole. The solution? Constructing this bridge, plus a long drive down to Poole Road. As an extra bird-flip to the council, Cordelia built a gate at the Poole entrance/exit, hung on piers like the ones holding the gate she'd been ordered to remove. *Ha!*

Deans Court is home to the oldest house in Wimborne, and has been central to the community for 1,300 years. It has only ever had two owners: the Catholic Church and the Hanham family, who have seen 18 generations live here over the past 470 years. During Saxon times, it was part of a double monastery, housing both monks and nuns. The fishpond that remains today would have fed the hundreds of holy inhabitants. Missionaries were sent from here to the Continent, and legend has it that two of these missionaries had a daughter who, in 853, became 'Pope Joan', the only female pope in history. Disguising herself as a man in order to achieve this role, she was single-minded in her mission. Much like Lady Cordelia with her bridge.

Address Deans Court Lane, Wimborne BH21 1EE, +44 (0)1202 849314, www.deanscourt.org, info@deanscourt.org | Getting there By car, follow A350, A349 and B3073; bus 13 towards Wimborne Minster to The Square | Hours Open to the public on specific dates (visit website for details) | Tip To the right of the fishpond, you'll see two imposing trees (an American swamp cypress and a tulip), which were brought back and planted by explorer Thomas Hanham, following his return from a voyage to the New World in 1607.

21_ The Dorset Bookshop

Buy some time

Tick, tock, tick, tock… No, that's not the sound of the clock-swallow-ing crocodile in *Peter Pan*, the White Rabbit's pocket watch in *Alice in Wonderland*, or Bridget's biological clock in *Bridget Jones's Diary* (although all of these books are likely stocked on the heaving shelves of The Dorset Bookshop in Blandford). There was once a time when eight clockmakers operated in Blandford, but that sound is actually coming from the English, French and Black Forest clocks dotted around this three-floor emporium, which looks like somewhere out of *Harry Potter*.

Kevin Cook, who owns the bookshop with his wife Denny, loves tinkering with clocks and often picks up some beauties at auction. Kevin has sold several 18th- and 19th-century Blandford grandfather clocks, although there's one that's *not* for sale. Standing proudly at the foot of the winding Georgian staircase, the 1775 longcase clock's dial is engraved with an image of horse-drawn carriages riding over Blandford Bridge.

As well as the captivating clocks, tens of thousands of new and sec-ondhand books, comics, magazines, plays, sheet music, CDs, records and old postcards on sale here, The Dorset Bookshop is also chock-full of weird and wonderful curios, including Chinese, German, French and English pottery, tribal masks from West Africa, unusual carved wooden items, sculptures, pictures, even Irish peat bellows. One customer was particularly pleased with his early 1900s Edison phonograph, complete with wax cylinders.

Housing their novel shop in a quirky 1730s building, much of which retains its original features, including some original paint-work, Kevin and Denny are proud of their old-fashioned ways. They encourage customers to browse, explore, take a seat, flick through. It would be possible to lose a whole day here; it's a good job they've got all those clocks so you can keep one eye on the time.

Address 69 East Street, Blandford Forum DT11 7DX, +44 (0)1258 452266, www.thedorsetbookshop.co.uk, thedorsetbookshop@gmail.com | Getting there By car, A350, A354, B3082, then left onto Common Lane and right onto East Street | Hours Tue–Fri 10am–4pm, Sat 10am–2pm | Tip Branksome Antiques also stocks an array of clocks and other intriguing treasures (www.branksomeantiques.co.uk).

22 Durdle Door

Where rock meets, er, rock

Shout, shout, Let it all out... If you YouTube the music video of the 1984 hit 'Shout' by Tears for Fears, you'll see the band passionately belting out these lyrics with Durdle Door – a limestone arch rising out of the sea – as a backdrop.

Durdle Door is located on the Lulworth Estate, which comprises 12,000 acres and is privately owned by the Welds family. Don't worry, though – they're very generous with their land and don't stop visitors from enjoying their vast plot. Eroded by the force of the waves over time, 140-million-year-old Durdle Door is said to be one of Dorset's most photographed and iconic landmarks.

It sits on the Jurassic Coast, which was designated England's first natural World Heritage Site by UNESCO in 2001. You can still see round ripple marks in the rock at the top of the arch, which are the remains of a fossil forest. This provides the most complete fossilised record of a Jurassic forest in the world.

The name Durdle originates from the old English word 'thirl', which means to drill or bore. To the west of Durdle Door, erosion has created a line of small, limestone islands called the Bull, the Blind Cow, the Cow and the Calf (who doesn't love a bovine theme when it comes to naming rock formations?).

And it wasn't just Tears for Fears who saw Durdle Door's potential as a dramatic setting: Billy Ocean's 'Loverboy' music video was shot there, as was Cliff Richard's 1990 Christmas number one, 'Saviour's Day'. Ocean by the ocean and Cliff on a cliff – how apt! The area surrounding Durdle Door has also featured in a number of films, including *Nanny McPhee*, *Wilde* and the 1967 adaptation of *Far from the Madding Crowd*.

If you want to avoid the madding crowd, make sure you visit between September and May, when the area isn't quite so chock-a-block with tourists.

Address West Lulworth, Wareham BH20 5PU | **Getting there** Bus X54 to Durdle Door; pay-and-display car park open 8am daily, closing times vary (check www.lulworth.com) | **Tip** If your boots are made for walking, yomp along the 630-mile South West Coast Path, which starts at Poole Harbour, runs along the Dorset, Cornwall and Devon cliff tops, and ends in Minehead in Somerset (www.southwestcoastpath.org.uk).

23 — The Earthouse

Once upon a time…

When was the last time someone told you a story? Not a '… and then I got stuck in traffic… so I was late for my meeting… and then a pigeon pooped on me…' type story. An actual *proper* story, with a plot, characters and a sense of wonder that takes your imagination to a place you haven't been since you were a child? This is what you can experience at the Earthouse, an extraordinary theatre inside a hill, held up by 21 huge oak trees. The 250 people it holds sit on tiered seating around a fire in the centre and become entranced by a professional storyteller and a band of musicians – think accordions, violins and 'body music' like foot-tapping, clapping, finger-clicking and shushing. There are no props, no special effects, no costumes… just good, old-fashioned storytelling. And it's utterly transfixing.

These 'Fairytales for Grown-ups' are run by The Crick Crack Club, which organises storytelling events up and down the country. The term 'crick crack' originates from French-speaking Caribbean countries, like Haiti and Guadeloupe. Those who are about to tell a story shout, 'Crick!' and, in response, the audience shout, 'Crack!'.

The Earthouse is part of the Ancient Technology Centre, which has six full-sized reconstructions of bygone buildings, including a Viking longhouse, a Saxon workshop and a Roman forge. It also has a Roman water-lifting machine, which has featured on *Time Team* and has completed 5,404 rotations, resulting in 340 tons of water being moved.

It's the atmosphere inside the Earthouse as much as the enthralling storytelling that creates the magic. It just wouldn't be the same in a regular theatre. The cracking of the fire, the flicker of the lanterns, the stars you can spot through the hole in the earthen roof all combine with the story to bring it to life. A word to the wise, though: your mind will enjoy the experience more than your bottom. Take a cushion.

Address The Ancient Technology Centre, Damerham Road, Cranborne BH21 5RP, +44 (0)7791 157437, www.crickcrackclub.com/earthousecranborne, kate@crickcrackclub.com | **Getting there** By car, A350, A349, B3074 and B3078, Wimborne Street (Wimborne Street veers right and becomes Crane Street); park around here and walk to the venue | **Tip** Music events are also held at the Earthouse, organised by Jam In A Round (www.jaminaround.com).

24 English Oak Vineyard

Be transported to cloud wine

What do you plan to do in your retirement? Read more? Garden? Enjoy some wine? If you were Andrew and Sarah Pharoah, you'd do all three… and then some. Having made their money in IT, they weren't quite ready to hang up their hats so, inspired by a Cypriot winery, they enrolled in a viticulture course, bought a 23-acre farm in the Dorset countryside and, in 2007, got to work ploughing, planting, pruning and picking the fruits of their (intensive) labour from their 23,000 vines.

They specialise in sparkling wine; the soil and microclimate (the vineyard is in a bowl with a south-facing slope) lend themselves to producing a high-quality fizz. Indeed, the conditions here are similar to those of the Champagne region in France. The three varieties of grapes grown – chardonnay, pinot noir and pinot meunier – produce three white wines and one rosé, each named after a type of oak: Engelmann Cuvee, San Gabriel, Wainscot and Chinkapin (Sarah enjoys the onomatopoeia of this – like glasses being 'chinked'). The 350-year-old oak tree sitting at the heart of the property is how the vineyard got its name, and guests are invited to laze under it during a Vineyard Picnic tour.

The Pharoahs are at the mercy of the elements – in the 13 years they've been doing this, they've experienced both the hottest and wettest summers in 150 years, the coldest winter in 50 years, and the coldest spring in 100 years. Hence their grape yield can vary wildly from 7 tonnes in a bad year (2016) to 86.5 tonnes in an excellent year (2018). It takes six years from planting to pouring: three years for the grapes to grow and another three to ferment, blend, riddle and rest the wine. Only after this are English Oak wines ready for the world. They are offered in 50 local restaurants and hotels, including The Pig on the Beach, Harbour Heights, Rick Stein and Maison Sax. Is it wine o'clock yet?

Address Flowers Drove, Lytchett Matravers BH16 6BX, +44 (0)1258 858205, www.englishoakvineyard.co.uk, info@englishoakvineyard.com | Getting there By car, A350 and Wimborne Road, then follow the vineyard's signpost | Hours Tours Fri & Sat during June–Sept | Tip Another local vineyard is Setley Ridge Vineyard, near the New Forest (www.setleyridge.co.uk).

25 Fame Ship Rudder

This man is wrecked

Tom Selleck… Charlie Chaplin… Salvador Dali: all famous for – among other things – their moustaches. Now we can add this guy, found resting atop the 28-foot wooden rudder of a 17th-century Dutch merchant ship, to the list. It was common for such ships to have rudders with carved tops, usually with a human or animal head. Shall we call this one Woody?

The wreck was discovered in a sand and shingle bank outside Poole Harbour in 2004, and was finally raised from the seabed in 2013. Known as the Swash Channel Wreck, it was the subject of the largest underwater excavation, taking almost a decade, since the *Mary Rose* ship at Portsmouth in the 1980s.

Following the raising of this rudder, which had to be cut in two to be conserved and took three years to dry out, an analysis of the timbers and a trawl through the archives of the time (some 15,000 manuscript pages) revealed that the ship was named *The Fame* and most likely originated in the Dutch town of Hoorn. It was headed for the West Indies in 1631, using Poole as a pit stop, when it got battered by a storm and, ultimately, succumbed to Mother Nature's wrath. There were 45 people on board, who all made it to safety; since no one died, the ship can't 'legally' be declared a shipwreck. Despite much of the ship's contents being looted, over 1,000 artifacts were recovered from the depths, including barrels, pottery, tankards, wooden bowls, shoes – as well as four other baroque-style carvings in the shape of mermen (also rocking impressive 'taches) and cherubs. They are the earliest to have been discovered in British waters and among the earliest in the world. These rare, decorative carvings suggest that the ship held a high status. *The Fame* was also heavily armed, with at least 26 carriage-mounted guns, implying that it could have served as a warship. Deadly weapons… but not as killer as Woody's facial hair.

Address Poole Museum, 4 High Street, BH15 1BW, +44 (0)1202 262600, www.poolemuseum.org.uk, museums@poole.gov.uk | Getting there Poole Museum is near the Quay. The rudder is best viewed from the first floor, with the information panels being on the ground floor. | Hours Daily 10am–5pm | Tip Another nautical display in Poole Museum is the Poole Logboat, which dates back to 295 BC.

26 Farehouse Trading Co.

Feeling hot, hot, hot

It's human nature to set ourselves challenges. Some people train for marathons, some do Sudoku and others yet take up a 'chilli challenge'. More often than not, with a burning tongue, streaming eyes and the desire to time travel to before they'd taken a bite, they regret it. This is what happened to a pair of hotheads who bought a Carolina Reaper chilli mash and a dried ghost chilli from Wimborne's Farehouse Trading Co. The video of them tucking in went viral, with one of the lads crying for his mum!

While the Carolina Reaper is now the hottest chilli in the world, measuring 1.64 million Scoville Heat Units (SHU), the Dorset Naga held this title in 2006, with a laboratory finding it to be almost 60 per cent hotter than the one listed in the *Guinness Book of Records* at the time. It measures up to 1.22 million SHU and was first cultivated by Joy and Michael Michaud at Sea Spring Seeds Farm in Dorset, about 40 miles from Poole. In 2013, it also smashed another record when a five-foot plant produced 2,407 Dorset Naga chillies worth £900, setting a world record for the 'Most Chillies Grown From One Plant'.

Of the 200-plus chilli-based products that Farehouse Trading Co. stock, a fair few of them contain record-breaking super-hot chillies, such as the Hot Headz Satan's Sweat Naga Sauce. Other equally terrifying-sounding products on the shelves include Blair's Original Death Hot Sauce and Dr Burnorium's Psycho Onions Ghost Pepper (whose tag line is 'hallowed be thy pain'). Farehouse Trading Co. previously traded under the name Wimborne Chilli Shop but, in April 2018, it upsized and relocated next door to the old flour mill in Mill Lane. The owner, James Bryson, has fire in his belly for all things chilli, and is proud to produce his own hot sauce, Sidekick, and run the hot-sauce subscription club Flaming Licks. Because chilli delivered to your doorstep is so hot right now.

Address Precinct, Unit 7, Mill Lane, Wimborne Minster BH21 1JQ, +44 (0)1202 980990, www.farehousetrading.com, hello@farehousetrading.com | **Getting there** By car, A350, A349 and B3073 to East Borough, turn left onto Mill Lane | **Hours** Mon–Sat 9am–5pm | **Tip** For the 'hottest day out in Dorset', head to the annual Great Dorset Chilli Festival and feel the buuuuuurn (www.greatdorsetchillifestival.co.uk).

27 __ Fenners Field Oak Tree
Really branching out

Aren't trees great? They help us breathe, they represent the seasons and, in the case of Fenners Field Oak Tree, provide a top picnic spot. The oldest oak tree in Poole, it is thought to be around 500 years old, which means it was alive at the time of Henry VIII's coronation and during William Shakespeare's 'writing classic after classic' years. It measures nearly seven metres in circumference, and supports a plethora of wildlife (oak trees support more wildlife than any other native British tree), including the caterpillars of the purple hairstreak butterfly, bats, owls, and deer, who munch on the fallen acorns.

A sweet chestnut tree in the grounds of Canford School (ch. 3) dwarfs ol' Fenner in the girth department, measuring 14.85 metres, and is classified as Dorset's biggest tree by circumference.

Poole and its surrounding areas are home to many other tremendous trees. There's the Remedy Oak in Woodlands village, just north of Wimborne. In the 16th century, it was said to have helped to cure the 'king's evil', a form of tuberculosis, when King Edward VI sat beneath it and touched people suffering from this illness. Hence the name 'Remedy'.

Then there's Beech Avenue on the Kingston Lacy estate (ch. 44), situated on the B3082 between Wimborne and Blandford, which saw 731 beech trees planted in 1835. Said to be an extravagant gift from the owner, William John Bankes, to his mum, there are 365 trees along one side, one for each day of the year, and 366 along the other, one for each day of a leap year.

There are also a couple of noteworthy local yew trees. One stands proudly in the churchyard of St Mary the Virgin in Lytchett Matravers and is thought to be at least 1,700 years old. The other is located at Bulbarrow Hill near Blandford and, unlike most yews that are usually found in churchyards and are managed, this one has been left to its own, untamed devices.

Address Fenners Field Recreation Ground, 26 Merley Lane, Oakley, Wimborne BH21 1RY | **Getting there** By car, A350, A349, A341, left onto Rempstone Road, right onto Merley Lane | **Tip** Tree of the Week (@treeoftheweek) on Instagram shows beautiful photos of trees from around southern England.

28 Forget Me Not Garden
Anything but garden variety

As you step into this delightful Victorian walled garden, you may half expect a mischievous bunny to scurry by, chased by an angry gardener brandishing a hoe. It does look like it could be Mr McGregor's garden straight out of *The Tale of Peter Rabbit*. You might not find any radishes growing but you may find seasonal French beans, red onions, shallots, tomatoes, fennel, sugar snap peas, leeks, black kale and flowering sprouts. The area was once the vegetable garden for the house next door at Downwood Vineyard, so it's going back to its roots, as it were. You'll also find an array of plants, flowers, shrubs, small trees, herbs, hanging baskets and garden ornaments for sale. A lot of what you can buy has been planted in 'showcase' flowerbeds, to offer inspiration.

The owners of Forget Me Not, Claire Goodhew and Terry Watton, are very clear that they're NOT operating a garden centre (which conjures an image of mass-grown plants lined up in alphabetical order – *ugh!*). What they have is a 'garden that sells plants'. And not just any plants: carefully selected, unusual, only-ever-British plants. Stocking British plants is of the utmost importance to Claire and Terry, so that no diseases or pests can be brought over. There's an increasing number of 'plant plagues' that threaten to kill millions of British trees, with infection either being airborne or spread through the soil. In the 1970s, Dutch elm disease killed 30 million trees in the UK and, although restrictions such as plant passports (yes, really!) are now implemented, diseases are still rife. In May 2019 alone, 15 pests were added to the Department for Environment, Food & Rural Affairs' risk register.

But at Forget Me Not, you don't need to worry about that. Only concern yourself with what you fancy getting your green fingers on, and maybe selecting which slice of cake you're going to eat afterwards in the cafe.

Address Wimborne Road, Blandford DT11 9HN, +44 (0)7467 381445 | Getting there
By car, A350, at Badger Roundabout take the 3rd exit onto A354, at Two Gates Roundabout take the 3rd exit onto Wimborne Road. Turn into the driveway that says 'The Down-
wood Vineyard' and follow signs to the Forget Me Not Walled Garden. | Hours Mon–Sat
9.30am–5pm, Sun & bank holidays 10am–4pm (hours may vary in the winter months) |
Tip Downwood Vineyard is an eight-bedroom house available to rent. It doesn't have a
website but it is listed on many 'cottage for hire' sites. Oh, and it has a hot tub.

29__ The Forgiveness Window
If at first you don't succeed...

Everyone deserves a second chance – even, according to artist Sir Laurence Whistler, Judas Iscariot, the disciple who betrayed Jesus. The notion of forgiveness inspired this window, with a repentant Judas looking to God right before death, with the 30 silver coins he received for handing Jesus over trickling from his fingers and turning into flowers.

Having designed and created the other 12 engraved windows inside St Nicholas Church – all with the theme of light: sunlight, candlelight, starlight, lightning, jewel-light – Whistler suggested this altogether more sinister creation as the thirteenth window to the rector in 1987. He outlined his vision, explaining that the window could only be viewed from the outside of the church, and would contain 'a shadowy figure'. The church council weren't keen, but Whistler, undeterred, ordered a panel of glass and went ahead regardless. He completed the window in 1993 and offered it to the church again. They declined, so he loaned it to Dorchester Museum. In 2012, the matter was raised with the church council one more time and, unanimously, they agreed to accept the Forgiveness Window. It was finally installed in 2013. It may have taken a quarter of a century, but Whistler's creation got there in the end. Sadly, the artist never knew his window reached the church as he died in 2000.

He would have known, however, that the church housing his other exquisite windows was where the funeral of T. E. Lawrence – aka Lawrence of Arabia (ch. 16) – had been held on 21 May, 1935. Amongst the mourners were Winston Churchill, politician Lady Nancy Astor, painter Augustus John, novelist E. M. Forster and Thomas Hardy's widow, Florence Dugdale (search YouTube for the clip that shows some of these famous faces arriving at the funeral). Lawrence's grave can be found in the cemetery near the church, at the far end, on the right.

Address St Nicholas Church, Moreton DT2 8RH, +44 (0)843 886 8668, www.stnicholasmoreton.org.uk, info@stnicholasmoreton.org.uk | Getting there By car, A350 and A35 to Sugar Hill in Bere Regis, then B3390 to Hurst Road. The church is just inside the park gates, near Moreton Tea Rooms. The Forgiveness Window can only be seen from the outside of the church, around the side of the building. | Hours Daily 9am–6pm (4pm in winter) | Tip Visit The Walled Garden Moreton, a beautiful five-acre landscaped oasis, located next to the cemetery where Lawrence of Arabia is buried (www.walledgardenmoreton.co.uk).

30__Fort Henry
A wartime relic standing strong

Prime Minister Winston Churchill, King George VI, General Dwight D. Eisenhower, General Bernard Montgomery and Acting Admiral Louis Mountbatten walk into a bunker... No, this isn't the start of a joke; it's what actually happened on 18 April, 1944 – six weeks before D-Day. This 90-foot-long concrete shelter that overlooks Middle Beach at Studland was specially constructed so that these VIPs could observe Operation Smash, the full-scale rehearsal of the Normandy landings during World War II.

Thousands of troops took part in the exercise, which was to be the largest live ammunition practice of the entire war. Using live ammunition was uncommon in such a drill, but military leaders wanted the exercise to be as realistic as possible. They selected Studland because the sand and landscape closely resembled that of the Normandy beaches. Today, it's not unusual for the bomb disposal unit to be called out to deal with unexploded bombs that have washed up on Studland beach.

Unless you're a scuba diver, you won't have seen that beneath the surface of the sea lie seven Valentine tanks that sank during Operation Smash, drowning six men. A memorial for these soldiers stands next to Fort Henry, where poppy wreaths and words of gratitude have been laid. Prior to this, Studland's long, open beaches were identified as a potential landing site for enemy troops, so anti-attack reinforcements – such as tank traps known as dragon's teeth, and pillboxes – were put in place. They can still be seen today.

Fort Henry is now owned by the National Trust and its historical significance was recognised in 2012 with a Grade II listing. As you squeeze through its narrow passageways, you won't be surprised to learn that Churchill – perhaps thanks to his love of roast beef and Yorkshire pudding – apparently became stuck in the entrance and required some assistance to gain access to the structure.

Address SW Coast Path, Studland, Swanage BH19 3AX | Getting there By car, A35, A351, B3351 to Beach Road in Studland, nearest car park is Middle Beach | Tip At the start of the coast path to Fort Henry, pop into Grooms Cottage secondhand bookshop, where all donations go into projects around Studland village.

31__ The Grand Cinema

Lights… Camera… Bingo!

As months turn into years and years into decades, time has a habit of marching on. But the two women seated atop The Grand Cinema, immortalised in stone, will remain forever young, and forever highbrow (assuming the currently empty Grade II listed building doesn't ever get demolished). The figure on the left holding a lamp represents learning, and the one reading on the right depicts education. In recent years, the goings-on inside the building – with calls of 'legs eleven' and 'two fat ladies' – have been somewhat less highbrow. From 1978 to 2018, a bingo hall stood here but, affected by the indoor smoking ban and online gambling, it was forced to call time due to dwindling numbers.

This iconic building was originally opened on 18 December, 1922 (1922 can be seen on the rainheads at the top of the drainpipes), with a theatrical production of Shakespeare's *Antony and Cleopatra* on the tiny stage. The next day, its first film, *A Prince of Lovers*, was screened. From there began a 55-year run of laughter, tears, shock, suspense, wonder – and every emotion in between – evoked by the big screen. The cinema could seat 1,000 people and the auditorium had a sliding roof that was opened in hot weather. A scene from the 1977 film *Valentino* was shot here, with extras sourced from Bournemouth College sitting around Felicity Kendal dressed in 1920s garb. Other nearby locations that appeared in the racy film include the Russell-Cotes Art Gallery & Museum in Bournemouth, the driveway of St Ann's Hospital in Canford Cliffs, and Emery Down in the New Forest.

Many moons ago, a revolving globe that was illuminated at night topped the building, between the two brainy women. It was removed during the war in case it became a beacon for bombers. Other than that, the building remains largely the same as it's always been, both inside and out. A grand example of a grand design.

Address 40 Poole Road, Westbourne BH4 9DW | Getting there Bus 1 towards
Purewell, M1 towards Castlepoint, M2 towards Southbourne or 20 towards Strouden,
to Grosvenor Road | Tip Westbourne is also home to a more intimate (and still open)
movie house: the 19-seat Bournemouth Colosseum, said to be the UK's smallest cinema
(www.bournemouthcolosseum.co.uk).

32 Grange Arch

From Dorset with love

Warning: this may leave you shaken *and* stirred. It's believed that the world's most famous fictional spy, James Bond, was inspired by a real person – John Bond. And it's John Bond's relative, Denis Bond, who, in 1740, constructed Grange Arch, previously known as Bond's Folly.

The author of the James Bond series, Ian Fleming, attended Durnford School in Langton Matravers from 1914. Not far from here lived the Bond family, who owned three estates, including Tyne-ham (ch. 98). Lurking in the shadows of the family tree – perhaps while shooting villains – was the Elizabethan spy John Bond. The Bond family's motto is *non sufficit orbis*, Latin for 'the world is not enough' – which Fleming used in his 1963 novel *On Her Majesty's Secret Service*, and which became the title for the 1999 Bond film starring Pierce Brosnan. It's said that the motto was adopted by Bond as 'a bit of a laugh' after he invaded the palace of a Spanish King, where he saw it written. The Latin motto, with the family's coat of arms, can be found on the wall of the entrance to Creech Grange, the stately home previously owned by the Bonds. Fleming also used the names of other Dorset families in his Bond stories, including Drax and Strangways.

Grange Arch – a folly, or ornamental building with no practical purpose – can be found up the hill from Creech Grange. Like all follies, its intent was to amuse and impress. Before the trees grew to obscure the view, it would have been visible from the rooms of Creech Grange. Visitors, therefore, could be awed by the breadth of their host's land. Grange Arch remained in the Bond family for almost two centuries, before being passed to the National Trust in 1942. With its impressive arches, pinnacles and battlements, it would surely wow the achingly suave 007, who, in his own pun-laden words, might describe it as – *double-entendre alert* – quite the erection.

Address Wareham BH20 5DF | **Getting there** By car, A350, A35, A351 and Grange Road to Grange Hill. Park at Creech Viewpoint. While facing the Purbeck Hills and the sea, walk to the left and you'll find two paths. Take the far left one with a metal gate, which leads to Grange Arch. About a 10-minute walk. | **Tip** Ian Fleming's morning ritual while at Durnford School was to 'strip and swim' in the sea from Dancing Ledge, which is about a 30-minute drive from Grange Arch.

33 The Great Globe

See the world

Even Greek Titan Atlas would have to hit the gym hard before he had a hope of supporting the Great Globe on his shoulders – it weighs a whopping 40 tonnes. Installed at Durlston Country Park in 1887, it consists of 15 segments and is 10 feet in diameter. But it's not just the physical heft of this Portland stone globe – one of the largest stone spheres in the world – that gives it its power. In 1932, it showed itself to be worth its weight in gold in the advertising world, too.

As part of Shell's 'Everywhere you go you can be sure of Shell' campaign, which spanned 20 years, the Great Globe was one of the British landmarks that consumers were encouraged to visit (in their cars, therefore using Shell petrol). A campaign Don Draper would have been proud of, it established Shell as a leading company when it came to advertising. Other Dorset landmarks in the campaign included the Cerne Abbas Giant, Bond's Folly (ch. 32) and Clavell Tower (ch. 15). Graham Sutherland created the Great Globe poster, which was his first professional commission as an artist. This helped to launch his career and he went on to design one of the world's largest tapestries, *Christ in Glory in the Tetramorph*, which is hung in Coventry Cathedral.

Look closely at the Great Globe and you'll see that it shows the world from a rather Victorian point of view. The British Empire is made to look much larger than it actually was; former British colonies South Africa and Sudan look like they cover most of Africa! At points surrounding the globe, you'll see eight large stone blocks engraved with the points of the compass. You'll also see facts and figures about the sun, the moon, the stars and Earth, as well as quotations from poems and the Bible carved into stone plaques. Reading them may inspire the notion that you have the world at your fingertips. If not, you could always just go over and touch the globe.

Address Durlston Country Park, Swanage BH19 2JL, +44 (0)1929 424443, www.durlston.co.uk | Getting there By car, A350, A35 and A351 to High Street in Swanage, then take Park Road, Durlston Road and Lighthouse Road. Bus Breezer 30, Breezer 40 or Breezer 50 to Swanage Bus Station, then 5 Durlston Explorer to Castle Car Park. | Hours Always accessible | Tip Look out for the two 'graffiti stones' installed so that if people feel the need to scrawl on something, they can do so here rather than on the globe.

34__Guildhall Bullet Mark

Gunning for respect

Having been Poole's Register Office since 2007, the beautiful 1761 Guildhall has witnessed many happy occasions: weddings, civil partnerships, citizenship ceremonies… It has also, unfortunately, witnessed a murder most horrid. At noon on 21 May, 1886, Alderman Horatio Hamilton, a long-serving councillor and former mayor of Poole, was shot at point-blank range as he left a council meeting at the Guildhall by the severely disgruntled John Gerrard King. Three shots were fired into Hamilton's head and neck. One of these bullets struck the wall on the side of the building and, although the hole has since been crudely patched up, its location can still be seen (two-and-a-half bricks above the 'Market Street' sign). King had purchased the six-chambered revolver for seven shillings from Henry Farmer's ironmongers shop on the High Street (now W. E. Boone and Co Ltd – ch. 100).

After being left to look after his mother and sisters following the death of his father, King – who had recently been licensed as a harbour pilot – wanted to take on ownership of his dad's boat. Hamilton, who was responsible for such matters, consistently refused to allow this and threatened that King's licence papers would be withdrawn unless he paid £60 for his own boat. Unable to obtain this kind of money, King was convinced that he was being victimised and that Hamilton had his own hidden agenda. When he was charged with murder, King cried, 'Dead? Is he dead? Oh my God!' *That'll happen when you shoot someone in the head!* King was found guilty and sentenced to death by hanging, but the public became sympathetic towards him and the punishment was eventually lessened. Hamilton had been a well-respected member of the community and hundreds of people attended his funeral at Poole Cemetery. His death, however, posed many questions and inspired much debate around town.

Address The Guildhall, Market Street, BH15 1NF | **Getting there** Three-minute walk from Poole High Street, five-minute walk from Poole Quay | **Tip** The ground floor of The Guildhall is now an office where births, deaths and marriages are registered, but it used to be a bathhouse where locals would go for a soak if they didn't have a bath at home. It closed in the 1960s.

35_Gulliver's Farm & Shop
The local rogue who was dying to escape

Stepping into this artisan cafe, shop and deli (which you can't walk past without buying a giant homemade Scotch egg), you'd never guess that it was once home to one of Poole's most notorious smugglers. Isaac Gulliver, known as 'King of the Dorset Smugglers', bought this 90-acre estate in 1789 and, when he wasn't kicking back on his land (which now holds picnic benches, toy tractors, a Wendy house and a giant Connect 4 game in a charming orchard), he and his gang would transport gin, lace, silk and tea from the Continent to Poole Bay. He later turned his attention to the wine trade, storing masses of the stuff in vaults along the south coast. After his smuggling days, he went straight and even became a church warden at Wimborne Minster – although, during this period, there was never any record of payment being made for the communion wine!

If, like Gulliver, you're partial to a drop of wine, make use of the on-tap wine in the farm shop, where you can buy a bottle to refill with red, white or rosé, which change every six weeks or so. Gulliver's is big on being green and buying local, offering a discount if you bring a reusable coffee cup, selling products from around Dorset, and using as many ingredients on the menu from their 'biodynamic' farm as possible, including grass-fed meat. It also provides work opportunities for adults with learning difficulties or special needs.

Isaac Gulliver, on the other hand, wasn't so high-minded. In a bid to escape arrest, he once covered his face with white powder and lay in an open coffin. His wife led officials to his body, telling them he had died in the night. Triumphant, he escaped, and a mock funeral was later held with a stone-filled coffin. Little did he know that more than 200 years later, the sweet treats that would be served at his farm might leave others similarly breathless. The chocolate cake? To die for.

Address Station Road, West Moors, Ferndown BH22 0JG, +44 (0)1202 619891, gulliversfarmshop.co.uk | **Getting there** By car, take the B3072 exit from A31 | **Hours** Mon–Sat 9am–4pm, Sun 9am–3pm | **Tip** Take a five-minute walk through the woods, past the allotments, to Sturts Farm, where you can meet pigs, cows, horses and chickens.

36 Hall & Woodhouse Brewery

Badger Beer: the beast from the yeast

Hopping Hare, Fursty Ferret, Wicked Wyvern… The Hall & Woodhouse brewery is certainly into alliteration when it comes to naming its Badger Beers (see!). It's also into taking inspiration for every one of its beers from Dorset – be it the beautiful countryside, a captivating tale or a mythical legend. In the 18th century, beer was drunk by everyone – men, women, children… maybe even thirsty dogs. It was superior to water, mainly because it didn't kill you – contaminated water could strike you down with cholera or dysentery. Charles Hall saw an opportunity and opened Hall and Co.'s Ansty Brewery (near Dorchester) in 1777. Fast-forward nearly 250 years and the brewery has been relocated (to Blandford), renamed (following the marriage of Edward Woodhouse and Charles Hall's granddaughter in 1847), and revamped (an £18.5-million overhaul around 2012 saw to that).

It is now run by the seventh generation of the Woodhouse family, can brew an average of 124,000 pints of beer a week, and operates around 200 pubs. It even employs a beer sommelier, who can suggest a meal at the brewery restaurant to accompany your beer. It also hosts an annual beer festival in June, which raises thousands for charity, proving that, yes, they can organise a piss-up in a brewery.

Badger Beer is the second-oldest trademark in the UK, being registered shortly after Bass in 1875. Tours of the brewery are great even for those who aren't beer lovers, walking guests through the fascinating beer-brewing process, using fun words like 'whirlpooling', 'sparging' and 'fuggles' to explain what they're witnessing. They are invited to taste different malts, smell various hops and try the beers. While beer is the brewery's bread and butter, it also produces the soft drink Rio, and made Panda Pops (more alliteration!) from 1968 to 2005. All in all, a bloody brilliant Blandford brewery.

Address Blandford St Mary, Blandford Forum DT11 9LS, +44 (0)1258 486004, www.hall-woodhouse.co.uk, tours.brewery@hall-woodhouse.co.uk | **Getting there** By car, A350 to Bournemouth Road in Blandford St Mary | **Hours** Tours Mon–Sat from 10.30am, lasting approximately two hours (children must be 10 or over) | **Tip** The brewery shop sells all sorts of Badger Beer souvenirs, including boxer shorts. Bottoms up!

37 __ Halsewell Mirror

Reflecting on a tragic shipwreck

Do you ever look in the mirror and wonder how all those wrinkles and grey hairs got there? Fret not; when you look at this mirror, you'll feel like a veritable spring chicken, seeing as it's around 250 years old. Once on board the ill-fated *Halsewell* ship, it now hangs above the main door inside St Nicholas of Myra Church in Worth Matravers.

The *Halsewell* was wrecked on 6 January, 1786. It was a tragedy that killed 166 people and shocked the country. So much so that King George III visited the scene of the disaster, and it's inspired many poems, paintings and an orchestral symphony. Charles Dickens' 1853 short story *The Long Voyage* describes the shipwreck, along with other famous misadventures at sea, like the mutiny on the *Bounty*. More recently, in 2018, folk band Ninebarrow (named after Nine Barrow Down in the Purbeck Hills) released their song 'Halsewell', which tells the story of the sailors' 'watery graves'. The ship had set sail from London, bound for India, when it ran into difficulty and, for five days, battled with whatever Mother Nature threw at it – violent gales, lashing rain, whirling blizzards. The conditions proved too much for the 776-ton, 140-foot ship, and it was driven into the rocks below a cliff near Winspit (ch. 111) around 2am. Some were able to scramble to relative safety and sheltered in a cavern or clung to what is now known as Halsewell Rock. Within an hour, the ship was dashed to bits. The cavalry arrived in the form of quarrymen, who hoisted 88 shivering souls up the 100-foot cliff using ropes and nerves of steel; 74 of these people survived.

As well as the salvaged mirror, in 1967 divers also recovered an hourglass, coins, cufflinks, cannonballs, a cannon (believed to be the one at Hedbury Quarry) and the captain's cabinet (which has been fitted in a house near the New Inn pub in Swanage). Haunting reminders of the power of the sea.

Address St Nicholas of Myra Church, Worth Matravers, Swanage BH19 3LQ | Getting there By car, A350, A35, A351, B3069, turn right and drive through Worth Matravers, the church is on the right | Hours Daily 9am – dusk | Tip William Jeremiah Bower, known as 'Billy Winspit', was one of the area's last quarrymen (he died in 1966). Visit the National Coastwatch Institution tower at St Aldhelm's Head, less than two miles away, and ask to look at the booklet of photos of him.

38__Hinton Martell Fountain
His tray runneth over

While this fountain may not have the wow factor of, say, Rome's Trevi Fountain or Las Vegas' Fountains of Bellagio, it still has a story to tell and water to spurt. Hinton Martell, near Wimborne, is the only village in Dorset – and probably the whole country – with its own fountain. It exists due to the determination of Henry Charles Burt, the owner of Witchampton Paper Mill, to have running water piped to the village in the 1870s.

Witchampton Paper Mill was the Paperchase of its time, and started producing paper in 1720, when it was driven by the power of the River Allen. It churned out cartridge paper, book covers, record sleeves, labels and other paper goods for over 250 years, until it closed in 1993.

The calm of this 368-person village is at odds with the origin of its name, which comes from Eudo Martel, the Frenchman who used to own it, and whose surname means 'hammer'. (If you want to wear baggy 'Hammer pants' when you visit the fountain, there's no judgement here. And, get this, you *can* touch it.) The village church retains the original spelling of 'Martel' after a campaign by Reverend William Barnard to restore the medieval spelling to align it with that of the town in France where the Martel family originated. The current fountain is a replacement of the original, which was intentionally built low so that thirsty sheep could take a slurp of water. The new fountain was installed in 1965 and revealed by Ann Sidney, the Miss World winner from Poole (ch. 42).

In 1905, Sir Frederick Treves wrote about the fountain in his *Highways and Byways in Dorset* book, saying, 'The fountain, of painted metal, tawdry and flimsy… No unhappy detail is spared: the ambitious pedestal, the three impossible dolphins, the paltry squirt of water, are all here.' Clearly not impressed, perhaps he should have taken a trip to Rome or Vegas to get his fountain fix.

Address Hinton Martell, Wimborne BH21 7HR | Getting there By car, A350, Broadstone Way, B3074, B3078 to Emley Lane | Tip Just up the road from the fountain is St John the Evangelist Church, which novelist Thomas Hardy worked on in 1870 during his 'architect years'.

39 Hotel du Vin Fireplace

Something fishy is going on

Some people decorate their fireplaces with clocks, while others might choose candlesticks, vases or framed pictures. Not Benjamin Lester. He opted for marble fillets of salt cod. Why? As a reminder of how he and his family became so stinking rich. Originally built in 1776, Hotel du Vin was then known as the Mansion House, and was the home of Benjamin Lester – head of one of the merchant families who found wealth through the Newfoundland trade. The unconventional fireplace lives in the hotel's 'Port' meeting room.

Cod sustained Poole's 'golden age' in the 18th century. Every spring, ships would leave Poole for Newfoundland, where they exchanged goods for salt cod, other fish and seal products. They would then head to the West Indies or the Mediterranean, where they'd sell the salt cod and return to Poole with stacks of goodies such as wine, fruit, olive oil, salt and molasses. There were a few families who dominated Poole's Newfoundland trade: the Lesters, the Whites and the Slades. Benjamin Lester owned 30 ships, and Samuel White left £200,000 (equivalent to about £13 million today) in his will. That's a lotta cod! These families controlled Poole's economic and political life for nearly 200 years.

The lure of the cod was strong, and many Poole residents emigrated to Newfoundland. Local links remain to this day, with around 30 per cent of Newfoundlanders claiming to have ancestors in Dorset. Many people from Newfoundland visit Poole to research their family tree, and are often thrilled to come across Newfoundland Drive and Labrador Drive (ch. 61), both located near Poole Quay.

When you visit Hotel du Vin to check out the marble marvel, why not head under the wine-glass chandelier in the lobby to the bar – giving the strip-poker-playing sailors on the mural a wink as you go by – and order yourself a nice glass of chilled Chardonnay? It goes great with cod.

Address The Quay, Thames Street, BH15 1JN, +44 (0)1305 819027, www.hotelduvin.com/locations/poole | Getting there 12-minute walk from Poole Bus Station | Tip Hankering for seafood now? Pop along to Storm, an award-winning fish restaurant on Poole Quay (www.stormfish.co.uk).

40_ J. R. R. Tolkien's Plot

He liked it, so he put a ring on it

Boy meets elf. Elf's father sets an impossible task for boy. Boy attempts impossible task. Boy gets hand bitten off by werewolf. Boy and elf die. Then are resurrected by 'keeper of the souls of elves'. Elf is granted mortality and the couple live happily ever after. Until they don't.

As love stories go, it's certainly not the most conventional. But neither was its creator, John Ronald Reuel Tolkien, more commonly known as J. R. R. Tolkien, who most famously wrote *The Hobbit* and *The Lord of the Rings*. His characters, Beren and Luthien, live (and die) out the abridged story outlined above, and a physical reminder of their ill-fated love can be seen at 19 Lakeside Road in Branksome Park.

Tired of his fame in Oxford, Tolkien retired to Poole in 1968 with his wife, Edith. She was the inspiration for Luthien after a lovestruck Tolkien saw her dancing in a glade, just as Luthien does when Beren spies her for the first time.

Tolkien and his elfin wife of more than 50 years lived in the three-bedroom bungalow here until Edith's death in 1971. In 2008, the house (called Woodridings) was demolished and two modern, four-bedroom family homes were built in its place. Interestingly, even though they are now on different plots, they both retain the number 19 – one called 'Beren House' and the other 'Luthien House'. Tolkien died at the age of 81 in 1973; he and Edith are buried together in Wolvercote Cemetery in Oxford. On their gravestone, 'Beren' is written under his name and 'Luthien' under Edith's.

In the 1950s and 1960s, the couple regularly stayed at the Hotel Miramar on Bournemouth's East Cliff. It was here, in 1969, that Tolkien signed over the film rights to his high-fantasy books for £100,000 while Edith played cards with friends. *The Hobbit* and *The Lord of the Rings* franchise has since grossed around £4.8 billion at global box offices. Precious, indeed.

Address 19 Lakeside Road, Branksome Park BH13 6LS | Getting there Bus 50 towards Bournemouth to Westminster Road | Tip Some of Tolkien's wise words – 'Not all those who wander are lost' – can be found embedded into Old Christchurch Road (at the bottom of Yelverton Road) in Bournemouth Town Centre.

41_Jerk Shak
Spice is the variety of life

'What I miss living in the country is you can't get decent jerk chicken anywhere.' Inside the very British Scott Arms pub is a framed picture with this quip and a drawing of a man and woman drinking tea, with the title 'Scenes You Seldom See'. Outside the same pub, in the beer garden overlooking Corfe Castle, is the Jerk Shak, where you can get the aforementioned jerk chicken. You can also get jerk pork, jerk prawns, jerk lobster and jerk wings, as well as callaloo (a sort of Jamaican spinach), rice and peas, fried plantain, a potent homemade rum punch and Red Stripe Jamaican Lager on tap. The Jerk Shak promises the taste of Jamaica in Dorset, with it aptly being located in the village of Kingston. Co-owner Nicki is originally from Jamaica and brings her family's traditional recipes to the Jerk Shak, which couldn't contrast more to the fare served at The Scott Arms – think bangers and mash, Sunday roasts and other classic pub grub.

While the Jerk Shak was featured on BBC1's *Countryfile*, Kingston and its vicinity has also enjoyed its fair share of fame over the years. In 1965, *Hereward the Wake* was filmed in Kingston, as was *The Three Musketeers* in 1966; in 1970, *Little Women* was shot at nearby Encombe Estate; and in 1977, *The Mayor of Casterbridge* was filmed in The Purbecks. On the walls of The Scott Arms hang photographs from these TV series, some with autographs from the cast. In the beer garden is an authentic-looking gravestone reading *Michael Henchard 1807–1852. Formerly Mayor of Casterbridge*. Don't worry, though, you won't be tucking into your jerk chicken next to a buried corpse – it is, in fact, a prop from the filming days of the 1970s.

If the Jerk Shak whets your appetite for some chilled reggae tunes, head to the annual Wilkswood Reggae Festival, which provides some multicultural, cross-generational vibes in the Purbeck countryside. One love!

Address The Scott Arms, West Street, Kingston, Wareham BH20 5LH, +44(0)1929 480270, www.thescottarms.com/jerkshak, info@thescottarms.com | Getting there By car, A350, A35, A351, B3069 to Kingston | Hours Open most weekends between June and Sept (weather permitting) | Tip Just up the road is St James' Church Kingston, which is known as the 'Cathedral of the Purbecks' due to its size and lavish decorations. It took six years to build and cost the equivalent of about £8 million.

42__Kent Road

Didn't she do well!

Where would you say the most beautiful women in the world hail from? Brazil? Thailand? Italy? Well, the answer has twice been the UK. More specifically, Poole. Out of all five Miss Worlds from the UK, Poole can boast two winners – Ann Sidney (1964) and Sarah-Jane Hutt (1983). Ann Sidney grew up in a house on Kent Road (near Branksome Rec), and this is where her proud parents watched their 10-inch black-and-white TV, on 12 November – along with the other 27.5 million viewers in the UK – to see their daughter take the crown. As Ann was announced the winner, pandemonium broke out in the house, with ecstatic hugs aplenty being shared. It was an open house until the early hours, with friends and neighbours popping in to offer their congratulations.

From that day on, Ann was catapulted into stardom. By Christmas, she was in Vietnam as part of Bob Hope's show for the American troops. Prior to this, her experience of 'overseas travel' was taking the ferry to the Isle of Wight. She became the global ambassador for the International Wool Secretariat, for which she earned £30,000 – considerably more than the 30 shillings a week she'd been earning as a hairdresser in Bournemouth. Ann moved on to acting, being in shows such as *The Avengers* and *Are You Being Served?*, and featuring in films alongside Mick Jagger and Susannah York.

At the age of 19, Ann embarked on an 18-month love affair with television entertainer Bruce Forsyth, who was then 35 (it seems he was playing a *Generation Game* of his own). Ever the romantic, a photo of him welcoming Ann at Bournemouth's Hurn Airport with a butler and champagne appeared in the newspapers. His wife wasn't happy! Neither was Ann's dad! Which is why Bruce visited the family home on Kent Road to explain himself and apologise for any embarrassment that he may have caused. Brucie always did know how to play his cards right.

Address Branksome, BH12 2EG | **Getting there** Bus 17 towards Bournemouth to Northmere Road, or bus 15 towards Bournemouth Hospital to Gateway Church | **Tip** Poole Museum's cafe has a large coat of arms displayed on its balcony. Guess who the mermaid's face is modelled on? Ann Sidney herself!

43 Keyneston Mill
Making scents of botanicals

Ever wondered why perfume is so expensive? It's just smelly water, right? Wrong! Come away from a tour at Keyneston Mill, home of luxury Parterre Fragrances, and you'll have a nose full of wonderful aromas and a head full of information.

The whole operation at this 'perfume farm' is like one big lovely-smelling experiment. The team plant, nurture and harvest over 1,000 varieties of flowers, herbs and other plants in order to distil them and extract the oil for use as notes in the fragrances they produce. So far – after much trial and error – they have composed four perfumes (and counting).

Run of the River, named after the River Stour that flows through the 50-acre estate, is fresh and citrusy, while A Tribute to Edith features rose geranium. This perfume was inspired by Edith Piaf's 'La Vie en Rose': despite the French singer's tragic life, she still saw things through rose-tinted glasses.

Each garden you wander around (with provided wellies, if need be) represents a different perfume 'family' – floral, fern or spice – and is inspired by something artistic, be it the world's first botanical garden, Orto Botanico, in Italy; the Bird's Nest Stadium in Beijing; or the geometric shapes of the works of Kandinsky (the gardener confesses this patch is a nightmare to mow). Take a moment to appreciate the water feature in the Fougere Garden, three mirror pools reflecting the surrounding foliage. *Mirror, mirror, in the ground… which plant/tree/ flower is the fairest around?*

What's been created at Keyneston Mill is delightful. They're using the English countryside to produce high-end perfumes, and also offer tours and workshops (one of which allows you to concoct your own fragrance) to show how they achieve it. At £160 for a 100ml bottle of one of their perfumes, it doesn't come cheap but, as with most things in life, you get what you pay for.

Address Tarrant Keyneston, Blandford Forum DT11 9HZ, +44 (0)1258 456831, www.parterrefragrances.com, events@keynestonmill.com | Getting there By car, A350 past Spetisbury | Hours Wed–Mon 10am–4.30pm | Tip For a real fragrant treat during the summer months, stroll along the Jasmine Trellis, then pop to the Citrus Collection, which contains weird and wonderful fruits like Buddha's hands and limequats.

44 Kingston Lacy Snowdrops

Take time to stop and upskirt the flowers

Every year between late January and late February, drifts of snow-drops bloom throughout this 40-acre garden, and it's been estimated you'll see six million (yes, honestly!) of the beauties as you stroll the one-and-a-half miles along Lime Avenue, up Lady's Walk, through the Japanese Garden and in the Victorian Fernery. It's in this Fernery that you'll see over 40 species of snow-drop. The subtle differences in size, markings and leaf shape may largely go unnoticed, which is why National Trust volunteers can often be seen (mostly at weekends) with a mirror, poised to 'look up the skirts' of the snowdrops to point out the contrasts to curious visitors. If such volunteers aren't around, you could use your smartphone's flip-camera function to investigate and take some 'snowdrop selfies'. You may notice that the 'Ding-Dong' species has a long two-tone green mark on its inner segment, or that the 'Heffalump' boasts a double flower.

Once you've had your fill of snowdrops, take a walk into the Formal Garden and Quiet Area, where you'll see the Philae Egyptian Obelisk, which was acquired by the estate's then-owner, William John Bankes, on one of his many trips to the Middle East. His extensive travels saw him collecting most of Kingston Lacy's antiquities and amassing the world's largest individual collection of Ancient Egyptian antiques – the most notable being the aforementioned obelisk – in the 1820s. Unfortunately, after being caught *in flagrante* with a guardsman in Green Park in London in 1841, Bankes fled to Italy, fearful he would face the death penalty as homosexuality was a crime then. To avoid Kingston Lacy being seized, he signed it over to his brother. Apparently, Bankes secretly returned to appreciate his former home and collections. Let's just hope he managed a walk amidst the snowdrops on one of his covert visits – it would be a crying shame had he missed out.

Address Blandford Road, Wimborne BH21 4EA, +44 (0)1202 883402, www.nationaltrust.org.uk/kingston-lacy, kingstonlacy@nationaltrust.org.uk | **Getting there** By car, B3082 towards Wimborne (the postcode for satnav is unreliable; follow B3082 and brown signs) | **Hours** Gardens open daily 10am–6pm (28 Oct–end Feb 10am–4pm) | **Tip** To see more snowdrops at the start of the year, park in the village of Witchampton (five miles north of Wimborne) and stroll towards Crichel House. Turn right before you reach the house and you'll discover the white flowers sprinkled alongside the stream.

45 Knoll House Hotel

Five go mad in Dorset

As a child, would you get lost in Enid Blyton's imaginary world of secret passages, endless picnics, smugglers' tunnels and lashings of ginger pop in the *Famous Five* novels? Turns out, the settings of these adventures weren't so imaginary after all. So, as a grown-up, you can now get lost all over again. Blyton stayed at Knoll House Hotel for many weeks every year throughout the 1950s and 1960s. She found that the landscapes, buildings and locals of Purbeck and the surrounding areas got her creative juices flowing – not least when she was swimming around Swanage's two piers (ch. 93) of an evening. Among the real-life places that inspired Blyton were Corfe Castle (Kirrin Castle in *Five on a Treasure Island)*, Brownsea Island (Whispering Island in *Five Have a Mystery to Solve)*, Blue Pool (ch. 101, the 'glittering' lake in *Five Go Off in a Caravan)*, and Clavell Tower (ch. 15, the building that 'brooded over the sea' in *Five Fall into Adventure)*. The *Noddy* series was another of Blyton's successes, and Mr Plod was inspired by the girthy Studland policeman PC Christopher Rone.

Blyton and her husband were creatures of habit and always stayed in room 40 at Knoll House Hotel, which has stunning sea views. They'd also sit at table 3 in the corner of the dining room, delighted to eat while gazing at Old Harry Rocks (ch. 60). Today, the hotel celebrates accommodating the woman who penned nearly 800 books that went on to sell more than 500 million copies worldwide. The Wardroom houses a bust of Blyton, with framed photos, book covers and illustrations adorning the hotel's corridors. Letters to and from her publisher and illustrator, as well as a signed contract, are also on display, as are all kinds of Noddy bits and bobs, from egg cups to paperweights, a tin xylophone to a ring-toss game (which features the now-controversial golliwog character, Mr Golly). *Golly gosh!*

Address Ferry Road, Studland BH19 3AH, +44 (0)1929 450450, www.knollhouse.co.uk, info@knollhouse.co.uk | *Getting there* By car, A350, A35, A351, B3351, Swanage Road to Ferry Road | *Tip* From a funny little man with a bell on his hat to an enormous man who lit his pipe from a street lamp: near the *Noddy* exhibition is the mahogany chair of the 8-foot-3-inch 'Bristol Giant', Patrick Cotter O'Brien.

46 Komainu at Compton Acres

Every end is a new beginning

If you ever come face to face with a pair of lions, one baring its teeth and one roaring, it's a good idea to get the hell outta there. If, however, they're made of stone and are in the Japanese Garden at Compton Acres, why not take a few moments to ponder their significance? Known as Komainu, often referred to as lion-dogs in English, the two statues symbolise the beginning and end of all things. The open-mouthed creature is uttering the first letter of the Sanskrit alphabet, pronounced 'a', while the closed-mouth one is saying the last letter, pronounced 'um'. Together, they make 'aum', a sound sacred to religions such as Buddhism and Hinduism – and often used in meditation to promote calm. The Japanese Garden, along with the other gardens in this 10-acre oasis, was constructed by Thomas William Simpson, a margarine magnate, in the 1920s. He had travelled the world and wanted to bring a bit of it back with him, which is why he employed a Japanese architect and workmen to construct one of the few genuine Japanese gardens in Europe. He imported statues such as storks, dragons, a Buddha and a laughing frog. This frog is perched on the koi pond, supposedly chortling at the evil spirits whose attempts to cross the water have been thwarted by the 'broken bridge'.

The Great Italian Garden, symmetrical in style, as all traditional Italian gardens are, is adorned with two authentic Venetian bronze lanterns and a statue of Bacchus, the Roman god of wine. The splendid garden was featured in Stanley Kubrick's 1975 film *Barry Lyndon*. The period drama won four Oscars and two BAFTAs, with the cinematography being described as 'groundbreaking'. With Simpson spending the equivalent of £10 million to bring his vision of a haven housing over 3,000 species of trees, shrubs, plants and flowers to life, this word could also be applied to Compton Acres.

Address 164 Canford Cliffs Road, BH13 7ES, +44 (0)1202 700778, www.comptonacres.co.uk | **Getting there** Bus Breezer 60 or 418 towards Sandbanks, to Compton Acres. The Komainu are in the Japanese Garden, under the thatched 'summer house' | **Hours** Good Friday–31 Oct 10am–6pm, 1 Nov–Maundy Thursday 10am–4pm (closed Christmas Day, Boxing Day and New Year's Day) | **Tip** Before you reach the tunnel to the Rock and Water Garden, notice the Wollemi pine on your left, one of the oldest and rarest species of tree in the world, dating back to the time of the dinosaurs.

47 Lady Wimborne Bridge

She loved structure

Some bridges you can go under, over or around without really noticing. This bridge, however – with its fine spandrels carved with coats of arms, scrolls and foliage – demands attention, much like the woman it was named after. Lady Wimborne, previously Lady Cornelia Spencer-Churchill before she married Ivor Bertie Guest (the 1st Baron Wimborne), was a local philanthropist. Not only did she set up Cornelia Hospital (ch. 83) in 1889, she was also instrumental in offering local workers a better standard of living with her Lady Wimborne Cottages (ch. 48). Philip Budge, the mayor of Poole, described her as having 'an irresistible means of getting her own way which should cause any man that did not agree with her to fly to the uttermost ends of the earth.'

This magnificent bridge was constructed around 1853 to carry the Southampton and Dorchester Railway over the main driveway to Canford House (which became Canford School in 1923), belonging to Sir John Guest – Ivor's dad and owner of the world's largest iron foundry. He'd only allow the railway to cross his drive if the bridge was designed by his architect, Sir Charles Barry, who is best known for his work on the Houses of Parliament. Lady Wimborne Bridge has some of the most ornate carvings of any railway bridge in the country (the central crest being the Guests' coat of arms), which reflects the power landowners held over British rail companies in the mid-19th century. Chiefly built out of Hamstone from Somerset, the underside of the arch is local stone. Trains ran over it for many years until, on 2 May, 1964, the last passenger train from Wimborne chugged to a halt. The line continued to be used for freight trains until 3 May, 1977.

Lady Wimborne was Winston Churchill's aunt. Let's hope he kept his wits about him if he ever visited here; when it came to bridges, luck wasn't really on his side (ch. 63), was it?

Address Oakley, Wimborne BH21 1QL | **Getting there** By car, A350, A349 to Whitehouse Road. Park here, then walk about five minutes to Oakley Hill: walk down the hill, turn right at the Stour Valley Way sign, go through the metal turnstiles and along the wooded path. | **Tip** Follow the Viewpoint sign (there's no longer a viewpoint!) and turn left at the top of the steps. Walk for a few minutes and you'll reach the River Stour.

48 Lady Wimborne Cottages
Charity begins at home

'This place is a pigsty!' Is this a mother's most-used phrase when encouraging her kids to tidy up? Charlotte and John Guest, who purchased Canford Estate in 1846, had 10 children. Ten! Charlotte's maternal instinct extended beyond her own family though and, appalled by the living conditions of the local farm labourers (many of whom had to share their hovels with their livestock), decided to do something about it. She set in motion plans to build what have now become known as Lady Wimborne Cottages, named after her daughter-in-law, who got in on the project. (She was also mother to a large number of ankle biters – nine.)

The first cottage was built in 1867 on Arrowsmith Road in Merley and the last in 1904 on Oakley Lane, also in Merley. Throughout Poole (previously part of the manor of Canford), 108 cottages and three schools (Broadstone, Hampreston and Hamworthy) were constructed in the same Gothic revivalist style. The one photographed is in Lilliput and was built in 1873. The light-coloured bricks, pitched roof with gable that includes an arrow-slit opening at the top, entrance porch, terracotta plaque of the Wimborne family coat of arms, and the ornate number representing the chronological order of construction (not the street address) all combine to give the properties the same distinctive look. They were mainly built as semi-detached houses but there were also terraces and a couple of detached ones. Each cottage had three bedrooms, a living room, a hallway and a scullery, which contained a sink, a fireplace for cooking, a copper for doing laundry and an adjoining pantry. In the garden, there was a small divided building, with both a privy and a pigsty. So, if Lady Wimborne turned up for one of her surprise inspections (during which she awarded prizes for the best-kept gardens and allotments) and uttered the words, 'This place is a pigsty!', that'd be OK.

Address 215 Sandbanks Road, Lilliput BH14 8EY | Getting there Bus 60 towards Sandbanks to Blue Lagoon | Tip Many roads have more than one Lady Wimborne property – drive along Oakley Lane in Merley, Lake Road in Hamworthy, Fernside Road in Oakdale, Poole Lane in West Howe and Blandford Road in Hamworthy to see how many you can spot.

49_Leatherbound Lion

The mane attraction

This resplendent chap is one of the 50 life-size lions that were created for the 2011 art project Pride in Bournemouth. They were designed and hand-painted by local artists, then placed all over town for locals and tourists to enjoy. Included in the majestic collection were Ted the surfer-dude in board shorts, Santa Paws, Britannia the patriotic lion, Shelly covered in seashells, the creepy Frankenlion, and the quiff-haired Elvis, Lionsome Tonight. Leatherbound was created by Lisa Berkshire, who was inspired by local literature and literary figures. Her lion features four authors: Thomas Hardy (who used the local area as a backdrop for his novels), Robert Louis Stevenson (who wrote *Dr Jekyll and Mr Hyde* while living here: ch. 84), Mary Shelley (who penned *Frankenstein* and is buried in Bournemouth's St Peter's churchyard), and Oscar Wilde (who lived in the area for a while). Wilde's children's story *The Happy Prince* is depicted on Leatherbound, as are various quotes from different books by these authors. Can you recognise any flowing through his mane?

During the summer of 2011, Leatherbound was fittingly placed outside Bournemouth Library in The Triangle (often referred to as 'the gay village' – you're welcome, Oscar Wilde!) but now resides in a couple's front garden in Poole after being auctioned off, with the proceeds going to the Born Free Foundation and Julia's House Children's Hospice. TV star Martin Clunes – a patron for both these charities – attended the auction event, along with actress and Born Free founder Virginia McKenna. The It's Got To Be Bournemouth lion, which became a memorial to Red Arrow pilot Jon Egging, after his plane crashed during the Bournemouth Air Festival, fetched around £4,000 at the auction.

With the impressive amount raised for charity, and the way they captured people's imaginations, this pride of lions certainly brought some animal magic to the area.

Address Aurora, 6a Lakeside Road, Branksome Park BH13 6LR | **Getting there** Hop On Hop Off bus towards Bournemouth to Branksome Chine, or Breezer 50 to Westminster Road. This is a private residence so can't be entered, but Leatherbound can be seen through the railings. | **Tip** The It's Got To Be Bournemouth lion is on display outside Bournemouth Town Hall from the start of British Summer Time every year, then goes into storage during winter.

50 Longham Lakes
The back-up plan

These two peaceful, hidden-away lakes are a wonderful place to escape the bustle and noise of everyday life. You can stroll along the paths, taking in the calm, and switch off from the world for an hour or so. But these two bodies of water aren't just scenic and tranquil – they could, one day, be a lifesaver. In the event that the local water supply from the Rivers Stour and Avon became polluted or unavailable, these lakes – or reservoirs – would step in. Or flow in, as the case is much more likely to be.

Previously a quarry (where some artefacts dating back to the Bronze Age were unearthed), in 1994 a huge operation took place to form Longham Lakes, involving the extraction of 1.73 million tonnes of gravel and sand from a 99-acre area. The lakes now store 1 million cubic metres of water. The cost of the project was £15.1 million, and around 3,500 trees were planted, carefully selected to provide food and nesting for birds. There are now around 180 species of bird around the lakes, including the great spotted woodpecker, kingfisher and Egyptian goose. Many birds, especially ducks, make use of a small island within the lake as a safe nesting area during breeding season.

It's not just our feathered friends who can be found in abundance here: the north lake has earned a reputation as one of Dorset's great coarse fisheries. It's teeming with 'double-figure' fish, with bream up to 18lbs, pike up to 20lbs, and carp up to 42lbs (that's about three times as heavy as a bowling ball). Cue many 'Look at the monster fish I just caught' photos of proud fishermen. Fishing day permits can be purchased from the warden.

While one of the lakes is specifically for fishing, the other is used by local clubs, including Dorset's Ultimate Canoe Kayak Squad, Poole Radio Yacht Club, the Christchurch & District Model Flying Club and Longham Birders.

Address Ringwood Road, Ferndown BH22 9AB | **Getting there** By car, A350, A3049 and A348 to Ferndown; the car park is reserved for anglers and bird watchers holding permits. Park at Haskins Garden Centre (BH22 9DG), walk down the A348, then go up Green Lane. 200 yards up there is a stile leading to the lakes. | **Tip** The Bridge House Antiques Market is nearby. As well as stocking an array of antique and retro treasures, there's a cute cafe inside (www.thebridgehouseantiquesmarket.co.uk).

51 Lush Cosmetics' First Shop

So much more than bath bombs

Love it or sneeze at it, there's no denying that Lush products have a distinctive, instantly recognisable aroma that wafts from its stores. This is largely due to the company's eco-friendly commitment to use as little packaging as possible – their so-called 'naked packaging'. This kooky cosmetics company was founded in 1995 at the 'wrong end' of Poole High Street – at number 29 – and this first-ever shop remains open today (although above the shop door it says 29½). Step inside and you'll be greeted with a 'salad bar' of face packs, looking more like hummus, guacamole and baba ghanoush than anything you should be smearing on your visage. By the till, you'll see Lush's exclusive perfume called '29 High Street', which mimics the scent of a Lush shop. Even though it now operates over 900 shops worldwide, Lush still likes to go local where possible. The seaweed and seawater used in its products are from Poole Harbour and Studland Bay (ch. 90), and the charcoal is from Dorset woodland.

In 2009, Lush opened a spa next to the shop, which promises 'transformative experiences' rather than run-of-the-mill massages, facials and scrubs. Indeed, if you book one, you'll feel like you've entered into Alice in Wonderland's rabbit hole, then become involved in a very luxurious science experiment (a multi-sensory massage with a side of dry ice, anyone?). Each treatment is performed to a different soundtrack – a combination of music and sounds of nature – created specifically for that experience. The spa's signature treatment, Synaesthesia, for example, plays melodies from a 52-piece orchestra and birdsong recorded from around Corfe Castle. CDs of the music – produced by Lush's own record label – are available to buy so you can recreate your blissed-out afterglow at home. The whole experience is seriously cool and seriously, well, lush.

Address 29 High Street, BH15 1AB, +44 (0)1202 672217, uk.lush.com/shop/poole, poole@lush.co.uk | **Getting there** 10-minute walk from Poole Bus Station, 4-minute walk from Poole Quay | **Hours** Mon – Sat 9.30am – 5pm, Sun 10am – 4.30pm | **Tip** If you want to continue treating your nose, pop across the road to the sweet-smelling florist on the corner, New Street Flowers (www.newstreetflowers.com).

52 Marconi Lounge

Radio times

Not all lifesavers wear white coats or burst in to burning buildings. Some unwittingly save lives due to their brilliance. Alan Turing did it when he developed a machine that helped to break the German Enigma code in World War II. And Guglielmo Marconi did it when his wireless transmitter was installed on the *Titanic*, meaning that the nearby *Carpathia* was able to arrive in time to save 705 passengers. Marconi was an Italian physicist, credited as the inventor of radio. His discoveries made radio communication possible, which lay the foundation for devices such as walkie-talkies and mobile phones. In 1931, he also built the world's first international shortwave broadcast station, Vatican Radio, which is still on the air today. His achievements brought him worldwide recognition and many things around the globe are named after him, from plazas to beaches, conference centres to schools. Heck, he even has an asteroid and a crater on the moon named after him! A little closer to home, Marconi Lounge in the Haven Hotel honours him.

It was in this very room that, from 1898 to 1926, he conducted some of his most important experiments. On the hotel's grounds, he erected two masts, one 120-feet and one 158-feet. He'd send wireless messages from here to his 'floating laboratory', his yacht *Elettra* (after which he named his youngest daughter). Marconi became friends with the van Raaltes, who owned Brownsea Island. They introduced him to Beatrice O'Brien and, on 16 March, 1905, they married and then honeymooned on the island.

Marconi Lounge displays photos from Marconi's time of using The Haven Hotel as a base, where he lived and worked. It also has cabinets filled with books, games and jigsaws. You could dig one out… or you could ease into one of the sofas and call someone on your phone. It's probably what Marconi, 'the man who networked the world', would have wanted.

Address The Haven Hotel, 161 Banks Road, Sandbanks BH13 7QL, +44 (0)1202 707333, www.fjbhotels.co.uk/haven-hotel | **Getting there** Bus Breezer 60 towards Sandbanks to Ferry Approach; Marconi Lounge is opposite the hotel's reception | **Hours** Daily 9am–11pm (unless a private function is being hosted) | **Tip** By the front gates of the hotel (on the ferry side), there's a blue plaque commemorating Marconi and his world-changing experiments.

53 Mathmos Lava Lamp Shop

Are you ready to get groovy?

Is your home crying out for a psychedelic adornment? If so, you may want to buy a slice – or swirl – of retro history in the shape of a lava lamp. Inside the Mathmos showroom and shop, you'll be met with a kaleidoscope of ever-moving colours. On display, among others, is the original Astro Lamp.

The Astro Lamp was the bright idea of inventor Edward Craven Walker, who founded Crestworth in Poole in 1963. Developed from a design for an egg timer using two liquids that he'd seen in a Dorset pub, he could never have imagined that his creation would become a world-wide sensation, attracting celebrity customers such as David Bowie, Ringo Starr and Paul McCartney. The current factory is near central Poole but the first one was located near Poole Quay. It then moved to Holes Bay Road at the end of the 1960s. The Craven Walkers were said to whizz up to the factory by motorboat or whirr in via helicopter.

Taking inspiration from the French sci-fi comic strip *Barbarella* (later made into the 1968 film starring Jane Fonda), the company is now named Mathmos after the bubbling liquid force under the city. Luckily, there is no such force under Poole... but there is the bay, which came in handy in the early days. Originally, Tree Top orange squash bottles were emptied into Poole Bay and refilled with the lava liquid. Of his invention, Craven Walker said: 'I think it will always be popular. It's like the cycle of life. It grows, breaks up, falls down and then starts all over again.' He was right. More than 50 years since its creation, via appearances on the sets of *Doctor Who*, *Superman III* and *The Graham Norton Show*, lava lamps continue to be hypnotically popular.

At Mathmos, no two lava lamps will ever be exactly the same. Each one is hand-assembled, meaning the ratio of coloured wax to liquid differs ever so slightly from lamp to lamp. Which one will you choose?

Address Unit 3, 19 Willis Way, BH15 3SS | Getting there By car, A350, Sterte Road, Stanley Green Road, Fleets Lane, Willis Road, left onto Willis Way | Hours Mon–Fri 9am–5pm | Tip Edward Craven Walker was somewhat of an eccentric and owned a naturist camp near Ringwood. If you feel like getting your kit off, visit the Rivendell Naturist Resort, where you're invited to 'dare to bare'.

54 Mayim UK Mermaid Academy

A shore thing

They say that if your thighs touch, you're one step closer to being a mermaid. But how would you like to get *even closer* to being this mythical sea creature? Enter the Mayim UK Mermaid Academy – owned by Michelle Forsbrey, aka Mermaid MerShell – which has trained around 800 mermaids since 2015. After a surfing and then a skiing accident, Michelle found herself doing physio in a swimming pool and, being a fan of Disney's *The Little Mermaid*, the idea of donning a tail to help with her recovery struck. The notion evolved and she completed various courses in order to fulfil her dream of opening a mermaid academy: she's a certified freediver, swimming instructor, lifeguard, scuba diver and, yes, mermaid (and has 50 bright tails – ranging in price from £90 to £1,500 – to prove it).

To obtain your own mermaid certificate, you need to complete the aquatic training MerShell provides, which ranges from Level 1 stuff, like gliding, twirling, tail-flicks and handstands, to Level 4 skills, such as life-saving and putting together a polished synchronised swimming performance. There's no exam on pirate seduction or preening oneself on a rock, however. MerShell has been honing her mermaid technique for years and can now hold her breath underwater for over three minutes and can dive to an impressive depth of 20 metres.

As well as hosting the Merlympics – which include events such as the relay, speed race, handstand contest and dive-down, which judges the most elegant tail-flick – MerShell also organises beach cleans in association with charity Surfers Against Sewage. They collect litter from the shores, including tiny plastic resin pellets, known as 'mermaids' tears'. But there's certainly nothing to cry about during a mermaid experience with MerShell. Her goal is to keep the magic of mermaids alive, and she lives by a simple motto: 'seas the day'.

Address Mermaid experiences are run at various local swimming pools, +44 (0)7714 991075, www.mayimmermaidacademy.co.uk, info@mayimmermaidacademy.co.uk | Tip Poole's coat of arms depicts a bare-breasted mermaid holding an anchor in one hand and a cannonball in the other. Spot her on various road-name signs throughout Poole.

55__Memory and the Tideline

Defending one's art

Functional doesn't have to mean boring. Like a pair of pretty slippers, if something useful can also look good, why not? Enter the 2001 Memory and the Tideline project, which adorns Poole Quay's flood-defence walls with art created by Simon Read and facilitated by stonemason Leon Russell. Read was commissioned by Poole Council to construct an art installation that focuses on the history and identity of Poole. He used a series of 14 granite pier caps to illustrate the notion that, in a marine environment such as Poole, all that is left on the tideline after the sea has ebbed is a memory. As with life, some of these memories bring a smile, like the Brownsea Island peacock feathers carved into one pier cap, while others invoke sadness, like the 'Omaha' one, reminding us of the thousands of troops who left from Poole Quay on D-Day (ch. 62), bound for the Normandy beaches. Some conjure amusing images ('"Twenty boys, mixed up like plums in a pudding" – Robert Baden Powell, Brownsea Island 1907'), while others are a little more highbrow, with Shakespeare quotes relating to the sea ('There is a tide in the affairs of men which, taken at the flood, leads on to fortune'). Others still are decidedly fishy, with bass, conger and turbot representing the rise and fall of the local fishing industry. Read's goal was to engage curiosity, rather than tell a straight story, while using texture to encourage touch. His work is subtle and could even be said to be hiding in plain sight.

One piece of art at Poole Quay that certainly isn't hiding is the 11-metre-high *Sea Music* sculpture. Installed in 1991, it was created by internationally renowned artist Sir Anthony Caro, who included stairs and walkways to allow people to get up close and personal to it. Like Memory and the Tideline, it was intended to be felt, appreciated and, indeed, remembered.

Address Poole Quay, BH15 1HJ | Getting there Memory and the Tideline runs along the front of Poole Quay near the water's edge | Tip Every summer, the Brownsea Open Air Theatre puts on a Shakespeare play on Brownsea Island (www.brownsea-theatre.co.uk).

56 Minnie Baldock's Plot

She gets my vote

What do A-list actress Patricia Arquette and working-class Minnie Baldock have in common? They both gave impassioned speeches calling for fair pay for women, the former during her Oscar-acceptance speech in 2015, the latter during a public meeting in Canning Town, East London in 1903. They were worlds and decades apart, yet both with the same goal: equal rights for women. Minnie Baldock was a suffragette who, along with Annie Kenney, co-founded the first branch of the Women's Social and Political Union (WSPU) in London. The cause for which they fought – votes for women – saw Minnie arrested twice, charged with disorderly conduct, and resisting and obstructing the police. She was sentenced to a month in Holloway Prison. While inside, suffragettes sent toys to her sons, Jack and Harry. In Jack's thank-you letter, he said how proud he was of his mummy. Minnie got a message out that was published in *Votes for Women* on 1 March, 1908, reading: 'I love freedom so dearly that I want all women to have it, and I will fight for it until they get it.'

And fight she did. She didn't stop fighting – touring the country with her megaphone, leaflets and tenacious determination – until 1911, when she became ill with cancer. In 1913, she moved to Southampton with her husband, Harry, and then later to Hamworthy in Poole. They lived at 73 Lake Road, and Minnie died in 1954 at the age of 90. Having joined the Independent Labour Party in the 1890s, Minnie left her plot of land to the Labour Party in her will, and this is where the Hamworthy Labour Club now stands.

Minnie's name and picture appear on the plinth of the statue of fellow suffragette Millicent Fawcett in Parliament Square in London, alongside 55 other women and four men who supported women's suffrage. Millicent's banner reads: 'Courage Calls to Courage Everywhere'. And what a courageous woman Minnie was.

Address The Hamworthy Labour Club, 73 Lake Road, Hamworthy BH15 4LF | Getting there By car, A350, left onto Coles Avenue, right onto Lake Road; bus 8 or 9 towards Upton, to Hamworthy Labour Club | Tip Both Minnie and her husband are buried at the nearby St Michael's Church graveyard (Blandford Road, BH15 4HR).

57 Nina Camplin Dog Mural

How much is that doggie in the window?

Who let the dogs out? Well, when it comes to *trompe l'œil* murals dotted around Poole and Swanage, the answer is artist Nina Camplin. This particular one, a memorial to Donut the Dog, was completed in 2002, shortly after Camplin moved to Poole from Luton. A savvy marketer, she included her phone number and website on the side of the house where it's painted, and has since recreated the scene three times. She's had more work off the back of this mural than anything else she's done – including various pieces for Swanage resident and famous TV/radio presenter, Jonathan Ross. The original was commissioned as a slight protest as the owners of the house were denied planning permission to put an actual window in. The house is near Swanage railway station, so Camplin has to retouch the mural every five years or so due to the emissions from the steam trains affecting the paint. Walk around to the other side of the house and you'll see a cat peering out of a 'window' from the top floor of the house. The human inhabitants clearly have a sense of humour, displaying a plaque that reads: 'On this site Sept 5 1782 nothing happened'.

After the success of this mural, Camplin's portfolio of canine creations expanded and she began painting pooches aplenty. In 2003, she teamed up with DogLost, the UK's largest lost-and-found dog service, which helps to reunite dogs with their owners. The organisation gave her a list of lost local dogs and she painted them on various walls of businesses next to 'Missing' posters with contact details on, in a bid to get these hounds home safe and sound. There was Henry on the wall of Lush (ch. 51), Mendie outside Storm restaurant and Chaos on The Studio Art Shop. Alas, these have now all been painted over, but you can see some of Camplin's other murals at Bowling Green Alley, Farmer Palmer's, Swanage Railway and Chococo (ch. 14).

Address 19 Gilbert Road, Swanage BH19 1DY | **Getting there** By car, A350, A35, A351 to Ilminster Road, turn right onto Gilbert Road | **Tip** Dorset Dogs provides a list of lovely places to take dogs for a walk (www.dorsetdogs.org.uk).

58 No. 67 High Street

Head(s) this way

If we want to discover new things, sometimes we have to change our view. The tour company Look Up London draws people's attention to objects above their eyeline. Perhaps there should be a Look Up Poole so that locals won't miss what's going on above them. Take, for example, the four terracotta heads on the 18th-century building above the Frontline Army Surplus Store on Poole High Street. Now somewhat weather-beaten (to say the least – one of the heads has all but fallen off), they represent four continents: Europe, America, Africa and Asia.

They were added to the building, along with the elaborate window arches, by the father of Job Loader, who lived in the building with his wife, Martha, and eight children in the late 1800s, and ran a yachting outfitters from the premises. Perhaps, with so many kids in tow, having 'continents' stuck to the side of his property was the closest he got to travelling the world?

Prior to becoming Frontline (which sells garments sporting slogans such as 'Keep calm and soldier on' and 'If you aren't going to stand behind our troops then feel free to stand in front of them'), 67 High Street was a hat shop, a dry cleaner, a bike shop, a florist and the headquarters for the *Poole and Dorsetshire Herald* newspaper. Established in 1846, the newspaper was launched by John Sydenham, with his son, also named John, as editor. The first edition came out on 9 April and was printed on the presses at the back of number 67. People were excited that Poole finally had a local voice. Sadly, John Junior died a few months later, aged 39.

In 1867, Sydenham's other son, Richard, launched his own publication, *Poole Pilot*, which promised to be more critical and cutting-edge than the *Herald*. It folded in 1869. The magazine may not have changed the world, but it encouraged the people of Poole to look at things in a different way, at least for a while.

Address Frontline, 67 High Street, BH15 1AF | **Getting there** 10-minute walk from Poole Bus Station, 4-minute walk from Poole Quay | **Tip** Another 'Look Up Poole' feature could be the rainheads on the buildings at numbers 87–89 High Street. The date of the original mansion house located there (1704) and the initials *S. W.* are included, which could refer to local merchant Samuel White or Poole MP Samuel Weston.

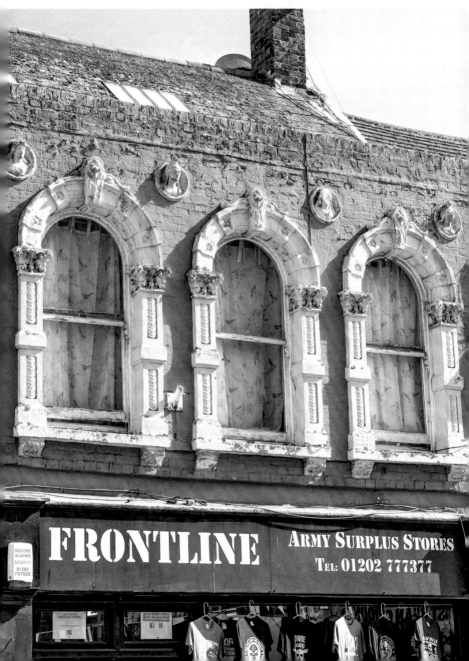

59 Oakdale Library Gardens

A secret garden with weighty tomes

This charming collection of award-winning gardens is easily missed. In 2013, a selection of dedicated library volunteers and Women's Institute members dug, planted, watered, constructed and went to war with persistent roots to bring the community-project – The Bookerie – to fruition. It contains an enclosed quiet reading area for adults, and a children's area where 'rhyme-time' sessions are held. Wildlife is welcomed, with bird feeders, a pond and an insect mansion. There are bright flowers and plants aplenty, which visitors can enjoy while sitting on one of the benches, many donated in memory of a loved one. Join the stone statue of a little girl named Rebecca engrossed in a book by selecting your own from the library, or look at one of the 'brick books' painted by local children, being guarded by a cute flowerpot man. Other reading material includes painted rocks, with sayings such as 'Reading is dreaming with your eyes open' jotted on.

Exiting The Bookerie, you'll walk past the herb garden, which encourages you to take a sprig (rosemary chicken for dinner, tonight?), to reach the Commemorative Garden, which was opened in 2014 to mark the 100th anniversary of the start of World War I. A poppy mosaic including the words 'Lest We Forget' is surrounded by poppies, crosses and red geraniums originally brought from Buckingham Palace. Every year a Remembrance service is held here, as well as other special services. The garden is a place for quiet reflection to remember those lost but not forgotten.

In 2017, a wonderful children's Adventure Trail was added, which includes quirky sculptures, hidden dens, string cobwebs, dream catchers, a teepee, planters in the shape of cars, and the 'Jolly Olga' pirate ship.

These gardens are only small but are an incredible use of space, and go to show that a little imagination goes a long way.

Address Wimborne Road, BH15 3EF (corner of Wimborne and Dorchester Road, opposite Poole Skills & Learning Centre), +44 (0)1202 674213, oakdalelibrary@bcpcouncil.gov.uk | **Getting there** Bus 6 towards Canford Heath | **Hours** When dry, The Bookerie is open during the library's hours: Mon 10am–6pm, Tue–Wed 10am–5pm, Fri 10am–5pm, Sat 10am–1pm. If locked, a library staff member will open it for you. The Commemorative Garden and Adventure Trail are open at all times. | **Tip** Canford Cliffs Library also has a pleasant garden, complete with pond and chairs (6 Western Road, BH13 7BN).

60__Old Harry Rocks

A novel place to end up

Old Harry Rocks refers to the 65-million-year-old chalk pillars emerging from the sea and marking the most easterly point of the Jurassic Coast, a UNESCO World Heritage Site. They began as a long stretch of chalk, then erosion made them caves, then arches, then stacks. British writer H. G. Wells – most famous for sci-fi novels *The Time Machine* and *War of the Worlds* – has been resting in peace alongside Old Harry since his sons scattered his ashes there in 1946. The small stack next to Old Harry is (*feminists look away*) Old Harry's Wife, who remains nameless. She is his second wife. He became a widower in 1896, when his original squeeze crashed into the sea. But like a geological Tinder, erosion has since hooked Old Harry up with a new 'ball and chain', by forming a new small stack. An advocate of women's rights, perhaps H. G. Wells and Old Harry's first wife shoot the breeze under the waves about the injustice of it all.

H. G. Wells once said, 'Beauty is in the heart of the beholder,' and, boy, with the striking, white rocks that gleam brightly when the sun hits them, does Old Harry behold some beauty! Did the writer know where his final resting place would be when he wrote the last chapter of his novel *Tono-Bungay*, aptly called 'Night and the Open Sea'? It concludes: 'We make and pass. We are all things that make and pass, striving upon a hidden mission, out to the open sea.'

No one definitively knows how Old Harry got his name. Some believe it refers to the devil ('Old Harry' being a traditional nickname for Satan), who would nap on the rocks. Others say a storm sank a Viking ship in the ninth century, drowning Earl Harold and turning him into a pillar of chalk. A third tale claims the rocks are named after Poole's most infamous pirate, Harry Paye, who would lurk behind the rocks, ready to ambush passing merchantmen, then stash his treasure nearby.

Address Handfast Point, Studland BH19 3AX | **Getting there** Bus 40 Purbeck Breezer to Swanage Bus Station, then bus 50 to Studland; nearest car park is South Beach, about a one-mile walk from the rocks | **Tip** The nearby Bankes Arms (www.bankesarms.com) has a wonderful beer garden with fantastic sea views to enjoy during the summer months; in winter, roaring open fires will keep you toasty.

61 The Old King's Arms
When Poole went to the dogs

Are you a dog person? The sailors and fishermen who docked at Poole Quay in the 18th century were. The Newfoundland and Labrador dogs they brought over from the most easterly province of Canada (Poole did much trade with Newfoundland: ch. 39) were not only calm, intelligent and loyal, they were also strong swimmers and excellent water dogs, able to haul nets, swim with ropes in their teeth and retrieve things from the water, such as fish and even people (a Newfoundland saved a drowning Napoleon Bonaparte in 1815). Captains saw pound signs in front of their eyes and began importing such dogs into Poole as a lucrative side hustle. The Newfoundland dogs were invaluable on land as well as in the water, pulling carts around town as an alternative to ponies.

Until 2020, this now-empty building was the pizza restaurant The Stable. However, it was once the King's Arms pub, which is where some of these dogs were sold. Reverend Thomas Pearce, who became an author on dogs, bought a pooch named Snow here in 1859. Another canine customer at Poole Quay was the 2nd Duke of Malmesbury, who saw Labradors' potential as hunting assistants, and began a breeding programme on his Heron Court estate at Hurn in 1823. Around the same time, the 5th Duke of Buccleuch was importing dogs from Newfoundland and establishing a kennel in Scotland. Years passed – *woof, woof, woof* – and a chance meeting in 1887 between the two families resulted in the Malmesbury estate giving the Buccleuch estate two dogs (Avon and Ned) in order to rectify the breeding programme in Scotland, which had all but ground to a halt. This is said to have saved the Labrador from extinction, and Avon and Ned are considered to be the ancestors of all modern Labradors. So, if you own a Lab, you've got Poole Quay's dog trade to thank for your head-in-lap cuddles, slobbery face-licks and chewed shoes.

Address 2 High Street, BH15 1BW | Getting there 14-minute walk from Poole Bus Station | Tip To see a different breed of dog in action, visit Poole Stadium and have a flutter on the greyhounds (www.poolegreyhounds.com).

62 — Operation Overlord Plaque

D-Day departures remembered

During World War II, Poole played a pivotal part in Operation Overlord, the code name given for the Normandy Invasion – commonly known as D-Day. This plaque, located on the side of the Custom House, commemorates this. Operation Overlord was the largest seaborne invasion in history, with some 7,000 ships and 160,000 troops involved. More than 300 craft left from Poole Quay, along with thousands of troops, making it the third-largest embarkation point.

Poole also provided several training bases, practice areas and shipyards that built many Motor Gun Boats and landing craft for the invasion – Bolson's and Newmand's shipyards worked around the clock to produce the largest number of landing craft in Britain. Operation Overlord was rehearsed on Studland Beach, making use of the Fort Henry bunker (ch. 30). In the run-up to the operation, locals recall seeing the vessels moored at Holes Bay, tanks lined up in Branksome Woods, and troops camped out in Shelley Park, Woodland Walk and Kings Park. Come 6 June, 1944… they were gone.

As well as Poole being used as a base for supplies to the Allied forces in Europe and being an important centre for the development of Combined Operations, it was also the headquarters of the US Coast Guard's 'Rescue Flotilla I'. This flotilla's 60 cutters departed for Normandy to patrol the invasion areas. Another plaque at the quay observes the kindness of the people of Poole to the 840-strong crew of these boats, who 'were credited with saving the lives of 1,437 men and one woman.' The plaque is located near Poole Old Lifeboat Station at Fisherman's Dock. The American flag displayed inside St James' Church (ch. 89) once flew on board one of these cutters, and was presented to the church by the naval forces based in Poole during the war, who attended the Sunday services here.

Address The Quay, BH15 1HJ | Getting there 14-minute walk from Poole Bus Station | Tip The Custom House has a restaurant inside called Custom House Café, which serves breakfast, lunch and dinner – as well as afternoon tea, coffee and cakes (www.customhousecafe.co.uk).

63 Packe Family Mausoleum

Where Winston Churchill was the fall guy

Located at the entrance to the car park for Branksome Dene Chine, the Packe Family Mausoleum was constructed in 1869, after the death of Charles William Packe. It was his wife Kitty's wish that he be entombed there. She employed Scottish architect William Burn to design the building and was laid to rest herself there in 1870. Burn was a sought-after talent and this modest mausoleum is listed amongst castles, churches, colleges, academies, manors, abbeys, country houses and monuments on his CV. He also built the Packe's mansion – Branksome Towers – which stood to the south of the mausoleum on the clifftop but was demolished in 1973. The mausoleum is one of the only remaining buildings on the Packe's 750-acre estate.

This vast estate was landscaped by Christopher Crabb Creeke, who became one of the area's most prominent planners (he now has a Wetherspoon pub named after him). He included features such as the bathing house on the seafront and a 30-foot-high bridge across the picturesque high-sided, tree-lined gorge of Branksome Dene Chine. This bridge was where Winston Churchill almost became acquainted with the Packes in the afterlife. In 1892, aged 18, Churchill was larking about with his brother and cousin when they chased him on to the bridge. Rather than be caught, he jumped, his intention being to slide down one of the pine trees to safety. Instead, he fell. 'It was three days before I regained consciousness and more than three months before I crawled from my bed,' Churchill recalled in his 1930 memoir, *My Early Life*. Before Packe died and was enshrined in the mausoleum, he had been a member of the area's local authority and helped to set up Poole and Bournemouth's first general hospitals to help the poor. Given the wealth of Churchill's family (his aunt was Lady Wimborne), it's unlikely that he convalesced in either of these institutions.

Address Branksome Dene Chine, Pinewood Road, Branksome Park BH13 6JP | **Getting there** Parkstone Road, Bournemouth Road, North Lodge Road, Archway Road, Leicester Road, Western Road, Tower Road West, Tower Road to Pinewood Road | **Hours** Ignore the details on the outdated plaque outside the mausoleum. For access to the building, call Poole Borough Council on +44 (0)1202 633633 and ask to be put through to Property Management. | **Tip** To see a lifesize wax model of Winston Churchill, head to Weigh In at 69 High Street. The owner of the shop was offered £10,000 for him but, alas, he's not for sale.

64__Paradox Comics
Holy comic book shop, Batman!

The wise uncle of a web-shooting superhero once said, 'With great power comes great responsibility.' For the past 25 years, the owner of Paradox Comics, Andy Hine, has seen it as his responsibility to fulfil all of Poole's 'Pow! Zap! Wham!' needs. As a child, while his peers were reading the *Dandy* and *Beano*, he was devouring all things superhero, lost in a world of prodigious powers and kickass capers. It was this passion for comics that saw him set up a stall in Poole's Old Town Market in 1994. Like the Hulk's muscles when he gets irked, Hine's loyal customer base grew and grew… and he eventually relocated to the current premises in 2005.

The shop is brimming with around 10,000 comics, with more in storage. Titles run from the mainstream likes of *Superman*, *Spider-Man*, *Batman* and *Wonder Woman*, to the more niche *Witchblade*, *Takio*, *Doctor Doom* and *Hit-Girl*. While you're browsing, you may also stumble across *The Walking Dead*, and be surprised to find that your favourite binge-watch show is based on a comic series. Ditto *Lucifer*, *iZombie* and *Outcast*. The most expensive comic ever sold is the *Action Comics #1*, which went for an eye-watering $3.2 million on eBay in 2014; it had originally cost 10 cents. While Paradox Comics doesn't hold anything quite so pricey, it stocks *The Batman Adventures #12*, which features the first appearance of The Joker's sassy accomplice and lover, Harley Quinn, and is worth around £250, if not more.

Hine, who has been referred to as the 'comic Yoda', is proud of the comic book community he's created. Over the years he's got to know his customers, their families, and the highs, lows and kapows of their lives. And they love him for it. A few comic book connoisseurs have even set up The PCG (Paradox Comics Group), which blogs, reviews and debates the crazy, cock-a-hoop, crash-bang-wallop world of comics at www.thepcg.uk.

Address 19 High Street, BH15 1AB, +44 (0)1202 661346, www.paradoxcomics.co.uk |
Getting there 12-minute walk from Poole Bus Station, 3-minute walk from Poole Quay |
Hours Tue–Sat 10.30am–5pm, Sun 11am–4pm | **Tip** Want to look the part while reading
your comics? Head to Geek Boutique, which sells comic book clothing, jewellery and
accessories (www.geekboutique.co.uk).

65 Parkstone Water Tower
Gunning for redevelopment

Aim… Fire! SMASH! Damn. If you were anywhere near the 19th-century water tower on Mansfield Road during World War II, this may have been what you heard. During this time, the Home Guard used the 50-foot structure both as a lookout post and to practise their rifle shooting. Unfortunately, they kept shooting people's windows out, so got banned from playing sniper. Locals also recall climbing to the top of the tower on D-Day to watch the Normandy-bound boats leave Poole Harbour (ch. 62).

This tower has long been out of action but it began providing Poole residents with their water supply after being completed in 1884 (if you have binoculars – or incredibly good eyesight – you can see this date written in one of the high metal circles). The cast-iron storage tank at the top has a capacity of 270,000 litres, which – at the present-day consumption rate – would satisfy around 2,000 people's daily water needs.

It is now a Grade II listed building, as is its near-identical twin on the aptly named Water Tower Road in Broadstone. Both towers were built in an Italianate architectural style, and it's been estimated they are comprised of approximately 400,000 bricks each. A similar water tower on Palmerston Road in Boscombe has been converted into flats, which is also the fate of the Parkstone Water Tower. Permission was granted in 2018 to develop it into a modern apartment complex, consisting of three two-bed flats in the tower itself, with a four-storey block of 14 new-build flats attached. Local opinion was divided – some furious about parking/traffic issues, while others welcomed the proposal, deeming it preferable to demolishing the decommissioned building.

Whether people were up *with* arms on the roof or up *in* arms about traffic, there's no denying that this Victorian tower has a fascinating history… and now, thanks to the new plans, it also has a future.

Address 12 Mansfield Road, Parkstone BH14 0DD | Getting there Bus M2 towards Southbourne to Uppleby Road or bus M1 towards Castlepoint to Castle Hill | Tip The Crusty Bread Artisan Bakery is just up the road and offers an enticing array of breakfasts, brunches, sandwiches, salads and flavoured breads. It also sells traditional Czech and Slovak products (www.crustybread.co.uk).

66__Pergins Island
Decamping to the bay

In the 1800s, parts of Poole Old Town were a cesspit of disease, filth and squalor. In the summer of 1849, the town suffered devastating losses due to poor sanitation and an outbreak of cholera, including the deaths of children as young as two. Thank goodness for Pergins Island, previously Doughty's Island. Sir Edward Doughty, the owner of the Upton Estate, which included this uninhabited 15-acre island, allowed the poor (and therefore potentially poorly) people of Poole to camp here every summer to escape the grime of their homes. It was mainly mothers and children, as the men had to work – but they'd visit when they could, bringing supplies. The tents were pitched to reflect the layout of their homes and streets on the mainland, and dwellers had to guard their firewood and water against theft. Doughty was a devout Catholic and, in gratitude to God for sparing his wife as she suffered a serious illness, he built Poole's first Catholic church on the site where the Royal National Lifeboat Institution (RNLI) headquarters are today.

As the years passed and sanitation in Poole improved, people were still allowed onto Pergins Island, now for holidays, camping trips and general merriment. Locals have fond memories of the place, one even temporarily converting it into a 'pirate island' with buried treasure for his kids. In 1980, Poole Borough Council took on ownership of the island and have managed it ever since. As part of Poole Harbour, it's a Site of Special Scientific Interest (SSSI) and Special Protection Area (SPA). It's no longer open to the public but is home to much wildlife, including rabbits, foxes and deer. Plans are afoot to encourage ospreys onto the island. A tree visible from Upton Country Park has been singled out that the council hope the birds will use as a perch.

The other islands in Poole Harbour are Brownsea, Furzey, Long, Green, Round, Drove and Gigger's.

Address Holes Bay, BH17 7BJ | **Getting there** By car, A350. Park at Upton Country Park and walk along the path leading from the first gravel car park. Turn left at the Poole sign, and the island can be seen from the wooden bridge (about a 15-minute walk). | **Tip** In Poole Old Town, there's a plaque (put up in 1904) on the almshouses on Church Street, stating that 'they have been devoted to the use of the poor for 500 years'.

67 Poole Flying Boats Plaque

A fleeting fleet

Between 1939 and 1948, Poole had a brief but historic moment as Britain's only international airport. It was one of the most glamorous periods in the history of air travel and little ol' Poole was at the heart of it. Having been relocated from Southampton due to the risk of attack during World War II, Imperial Airways' seaplane service moored up at Poole Quay. With all other airlines grounded, Poole's flying boats became the only passenger service in and out of the country – flying to South Africa, India, Australia and the US. Imperial Airways merged with British Airways and they began operating as British Overseas Airways Corporation (BOAC). This being the forerunner of British Airways, Poole can claim to be the birthplace of the modern BA.

This plaque is at the entrance of the four-star Harbour Heights Hotel, as this was the favourite accommodation for flying boat passengers, and where the stewards were trained in catering. Both pilots and passengers stayed at the hotel, where the panoramic view of Poole Harbour meant they could see the five main 'trotways' (water runways). VIP travellers included King George VI, General Charles de Gaulle, Lord Beaverbrook, singer Vera Lynn, and film stars Gracie Fields, George Formby and Stewart Granger.

There were more than 100 flying boats in operation, both civil and military, but three giant Boeings were particularly associated with Harbour Heights: the *Bristol*, *Bangor* and – Winston Churchill's favourite – *Berwick*.

The BOAC headquarters, known as Airways House, was at 4 High Street – where Poole Museum now is. There is a blue plaque similar to the one at Harbour Heights there. During the flying boat years – before they were moved back to Southampton – Poole saw 34,000 passengers fly into and out of its harbour, with the flying boats racking up millions of air miles. A heyday indeed.

Address Harbour Heights Hotel, 73 Haven Road, BH13 7LW, +44 (0)800 484 0048, www.fjbhotels.co.uk/harbour-heights-hotel | Getting there Bus 12 towards Sandbanks or Breezer 50 towards Swanage, to St Ann's Hospital | Tip The 'propellerhead flower' sculpture outside John Lewis in Branksome is a nod to the flying boats of Poole.

68 — Poole Park Pillars

The eagle eyes are always watching

What does this stone pillar adorned with sea creatures, scallop shells and an angry-looking eagle on top have in common with a flushing toilet? Answer: George Jennings.

In 1851, Jennings – then a sanitary engineer and plumber – provided the sanitation measures for the Great Exhibition in London, where more than 800,000 visitors each paid a penny to use the facilities. This is where the phrase 'to spend a penny' originated.

A few years later, Jennings turned his hand to clay, and the South Western Pottery, based in Parkstone, took shape. The terracotta eagle on this pillar – and the others located at the various entrances to Poole Park – were created by Jennings.

Today, these pillars are listed structures, thus deemed of significant national importance, as are the imposing iron gates of the park, the war memorial and the cricket pavilion.

Eyeing the majestic eagles, you may ponder what they've witnessed since the park opened in 1890. Rest assured they've not been bored atop their pedestals. For starters, there was the disastrous official opening itself, when Edward, Prince of Wales, arrived to do the honours, only for a gale to be blowing, leaving the marquee and street decorations in tatters. Last-minute plans were made to hold the ceremony on the railway platform but were quashed by police on safety grounds. In the end, a handful of people piled into the cramped booking office, where no one even bothered to make a speech.

The eagles also had front-row seats to the wartime German bomb that destroyed the bridge across the lake and killed two ducks; the tennis courts being transformed into allotments to help the government's Dig for Victory campaign; the Himalayan black bear living in the (now-closed) zoo; and the various cars that have accidentally rolled into Swan Lake over the years. Whatever will they see next?

Address Parkstone Road, BH15 2SF | Getting there Bus M1 or M2 towards Poole; entrances for cars on Kingland Road, Sandbanks Road, Whitecliff Road and Copse Close; by foot, main entrances on Parkstone Road, Sandbanks Road and Whitecliff Road | Tip The Kitchen, located in the middle of Poole Park, has a lovely view of the lake and serves breakfast, lunch, cakes and hot drinks.

69 Poole Pottery Tile Panel

Spend a day on the tiles

Once set on the exterior wall of Poole Pottery's factory facing East Quay Road, for the world to see, enjoy and, in the case of some local siblings, throw balls at to find out who could hit the woman's breast first (kids, eh!), this 1880 tile panel is now tucked away in the Dolphin Quays apartment and shopping complex. This was the site of the Poole Pottery factory until 1999, when it closed down for financial reasons and the business was ultimately relocated to Stoke-on-Trent. This panel, depicting Grecian students and their half-dressed, seemingly half-asleep teacher, represents learning. With the open books and globe, maybe it's a lesson in literature, geography and anatomy all rolled into one (or perhaps even home economics, as she requires someone to sew up her attire).

Another tile panel at Dolphin Quays that remains from the Poole Pottery days is the 1905 'Carters' one that displays an art nouveau lustre glaze which, in the world of pottery and tiles, is kind of a big deal, with Victorian potter William de Morgan spending much time experimenting with innovative glazes until he obtained this shimmery 'lustre' finish. Poole Pottery was originally part of Carter & Co., which counted the London Underground as one of its customers, providing much of the ceramic tiling for its stations in the 1930s. It also provided one-and-a-half miles of tiling for a chocolate factory in Norwich, plus tiles for London hotels The Savoy and Claridge's.

The two turquoise and dark blue tile panels at the front of Dolphin Quays, above the stairs, were originally displayed at the Carter & Co. stand at the Ideal Home Exhibition in 1927, then used at the showroom of the East Quay Road factory. The most recent tile panel at this location is the memorial that commemorates the 50th anniversary of D-Day, which was unveiled on 3 June, 1994. All in all, a collection of tiles with style.

Address Dolphin Quays, Poole Quay, BH15 1HH | **Getting there** Walk up the stairs at the front of the building, past Rancho Steak House, and the Grecian tile panel is on the right | **Tip** The Tile Lady offers tours around town, pointing out various tiles of interest (www.facebook.com/tileladyuk).

70__Pottery Pier
Smashed it

You know when you have an amazing idea, then you put it into practice and you realise it isn't so amazing after all? The creators of Google+ and Cheetos Lip Balm likely feel this way. As did ex-army officer Colonel William Waugh and his wife, Mary, when they bought Brownsea Island (the largest of eight islands in Poole Harbour) in 1852 for £13,000.

Mary had previously got her umbrella stuck in the sand along the beach and, when she pulled it out, she saw clay – and thought she'd struck gold. The couple set up Branksea Clay & Pottery Company (Branksea was the old name for Brownsea) on the south shore, with the intention of using the island's clay to produce fine porcelain china, similar in quality to that of the nearby Furzebrook clay. They went to town, constructing a three-storey pottery, complete with engines, brickworks and a horse-drawn tram to transport clay from the north side of the 500-acre island. The Colonel built a village to house the 200-plus workers, naming it Maryland, after his wife. He also constructed the church of St Mary the Virgin (probably named after a different Mary). Unfortunately, the clay wasn't as high-quality as they had anticipated, so they ended up making terracotta chimney pots and sewage pipes. All brownie points gained for naming a village after his wife were most likely revoked at this point.

Unable to sell their products for a profit, the Waughs filed for bankruptcy after five years and fled to Spain with huge debts in their wake. Maryland was used as a decoy in World War II, with Poole blacked out and oil tanks being lit here to throw German bombers off the scent. As a result, the cottages at Maryland were damaged and later demolished.

Today, the beach by the now-derelict Pottery Pier is littered with remnants of terracotta pots and pipes from the pottery days – like broken dreams scattered along the shore.

Address Brownsea Island, Poole Harbour, BH13 7EE, +44 (0)1202 707744, www.nationaltrust.org.uk/brownsea-island, brownseaisland@nationaltrust.org.uk | Getting there Take a boat from either Sandbanks by the chain ferry (takes about 10 minutes) or Poole Quay (takes about 45 minutes) to Brownsea Island. On arrival, you will be given a map that can lead you to Pottery Pier (30- to 45-minute walk depending on your pace). | Hours Brownsea Island is open to the public from Feb to Nov (check website for times) | Tip Fancy yourself as a potter? Take a pottery class at Furzebrook Studios. Perhaps try a bowl rather than a chimney pot or sewage pipe, though (www.furzebrookstudios.com).

71 The Powder House
A building that is bang out of order

Some things in life are never a good idea: sandals with socks, eating right before swimming, and storing gunpowder in the middle of town. This pile of rubble was once part of the Powder House, a building vital in keeping Poole from going *BOOM!* Here the town kept a stock of gunpowder ready and waiting should the need to defend arise. In 1775, following a shipment of six tons of gunpowder into the quay and a fire in a bakehouse nearby, it was decided that the town didn't need to see fireworks (it would save that for tourists on Thursday nights a few centuries later), so the stone Powder House was built well away at Baiter Park. Sailors carrying gunpowder were required to deposit it here before entering Poole Harbour.

The building was about 20 square feet with a small window, two-foot-thick walls and a huge studded oak door, only accessible with an eight-inch-long key. Had a big explosion occurred inside, the triangular roof would have been blasted off (cartoon-style) but the walls would have remained intact. Around 1900, when more reliable ways of storing explosives were being used, the gunpowder was moved out and the building left empty, until World War II when it stored munitions.

During outbreaks of disease and extreme illness, Baiter was used to isolate infectious people in temporary accommodation, and the Powder House was used for this purpose, as was the windmill, which once stood nearby and dated back to 1445. In 1837, the purpose-built Isolation Hospital was constructed at Baiter, which remained in use until 1936 (the same year as the typhoid fever outbreak, which affected 718 people in the area and killed 51). When the hospital closed, stone from the Powder House was used to block up its doors and windows to keep people out. The Isolation Hospital was torn down in 1963 and the Powder House left as a ruin, which is deteriorating more and more each year.

Address Baiter Park, BH15 1UX | Getting there Park at the car park on Catalina Drive. Walk across the grass and the Powder House ruins are by the water's edge, almost directly in front of the toilet block. | Tip The remains of the 1880s open-air seawater swimming baths can also be seen at Baiter (but only at low tide).

72 Pterosaur Skull Fossil
A head for politics

Fossils are a lot of things: fascinating, intriguing, enigmatic and, in the case of this 155-million-year-old pterosaur skull, political. Discovered in Kimmeridge Bay in 2009 by local fossil hunter Steve Etches, the long, pointy head reminded him of the caricature of Margaret Thatcher – the 'Torydactyl' – drawn by satirical artist Gerald Scarfe, so he and a fellow researcher named it Cuspicephalus scarfi. On display in The Etches Collection fossil museum, which holds over 2,000 of Steve's incredible prehistoric finds, the fossilised head of this flying reptile is the most significant pterosaur skull to be found in the UK for around 200 years. It is 326mm long, which is similar in size to the skull of a stork or heron. Scarfe donated the use of his 'Torydactyl' drawing to the museum, and it's been put on a T-shirt on sale in the gift shop.

Kimmeridge Bay is part of the famous Jurassic Coast World Heritage Site, which brims with fossils. Etches, who found his first fossil at the age of five, heads out to the bay two or three times a month (sometimes with Charlie Newman, the landlord of the Square & Compass pub: ch. 87), hoping for that adrenaline rush he feels when he unearths a new discovery. Some trips he returns empty-handed; others he may be dragging back a slab of rock as heavy as 63.5 kg by himself.

One of the larger fossils in the museum is the two-metre jaw of a giant pliosaur, a mega predator in the Kimmeridge seas. The world's first fossilised ammonite eggs are also on display, as are fossilised barnacles, like the ones Charles Darwin studied to explore his theory of evolution.

Etches has been adding to his collection for over 35 years and, when it comes to fossils, he's certainly been there, done that and got the T-shirt – as can you if you want to sport an Iron Lady/pterosaur hybrid on your chest.

Address The Etches Collection, Kimmeridge, Wareham BH20 5PE, +44 (0)1929 270000, www.theetchescollection.org, info@theetchescollection.org | Getting there By car, A350, A35, A351 and Grange Road to Kimmeridge. The pterosaur skull fossil is in the main exhibition room, on your right upon entering. | Hours Daily 10am–5pm (except 24, 25 and 26 Dec) | Tip Be a fossil hunter yourself at Kimmeridge Bay, a five-minute drive from the museum. Note that you can only enter via a toll road.

73   Purbeck Mineral & Mining Museum
Make clay while the sun shines

Had it not been for Purbeck clay, your nan's china collection would have looked very different. Josiah Wedgwood, founder of the world-renowned fine china company Wedgwood, signed his first contract for 1,400 tons of Purbeck ball clay per year in 1771. The potter and entrepreneur had spent years searching for clays that were as white as possible when he was introduced to ball clay, a rare, fine-textured clay found only in a few places across the globe, including Devon and Purbeck. He used it as a key ingredient in his creamware, aka 'Queen's Ware'. But using clay for pottery was nothing new. Clay has been dug in Purbeck since the Bronze Age, and the Romans manufactured it here on an industrial scale.

The Purbeck Mineral and Mining Museum (operated by Swanage Railway), which took over a decade and 30,000 volunteer hours to set up, was opened in 2014 by *Antique Roadshow*'s Paul Atterbury and MP Richard Drax. It's located on the site of the old Norden Clay Works, in one of the last remaining mine buildings, which closed in 1999. After you've learned about the history of the ball clay industry, the railways that served it (including Dorset's first railway, the Middlebere Plateway, which transported around 10,000 tons of clay each year), and the lives of the workers, you can make like Jamiroquai by 'going deeper underground' into the mine tunnel. Walk along the tracks which would once have transported clay-filled tubs up to the outside world with the use of a winch. The winchman and the miners communicated by pulling on a cable that ran underground. Yanking on it would ring a bell, and the number of rings gave different instructions: one ring for 'stop', two for 'haul up', three for 'haul down'... seven for 'have a beer waiting, mate' (note: this last one may be fictitious). In the museum, be sure to look up to see – and pull on – this cable. *Ding!*

Address Norden Car Park, Wareham BH20 5DW, +44 (0)1929 481461, www.purbeckminingmuseum.org | **Getting there** By car, A350, A35 and A351, at Norden Roundabout, take the first exit, turn left; bus Breezer 40 towards Swanage to Norden Bridge | **Hours** Opening hours vary, see website for details | **Tip** Outside the museum, follow signs for 'sidings', turn left into the field and you'll see Corfe Castle peeking through the trees.

74__The Quarter Jack
About time

Every quarter of an hour, this little man dings his two bells so confidently that you'd never know he once had an almighty identity crisis. Originally a monk, he was repainted and rebranded during the Napoleonic Wars some time between 1803 and 1815 into a grenadier soldier, complete with full infantry garb, including red coat, knee boots and tricorn hat (which was presumably added). Wimborne Minster used to be a monastery, and the monk was created in 1612 by a craftsman in Blandford Forum, who was paid 10 shillings. The Quarter Jack stands on the west bell tower of the Minster and has inspired a number of businesses around town to either take his name (The Quarter Jack Surgery) or his image (the estate agents across the road has a depiction of him hanging on the outside wall). The nearby housing development, Quarter Jack Park, opened in September 2019.

Inside the building, also in the west bell tower, you'll find an astronomical clock, believed to have been made around 1320, which is one of the most ancient working clocks in Europe. With the earth in the centre and the moon and sun orbiting it, you may think things are a bit off-kilter with it, but this is how people believed the solar system worked at the time. In 1543, however, Polish astronomer Nicolaus Copernicus taught us that we aren't actually the centre of the universe (although, alas, some people still believe themselves to be: #itsallaboutme). The sun points to the hour on the 24-hour dial, while the gold and black orb shows the lunar phases – when there's a full moon, it's gold and when there's a new moon, it's black (with varying degrees of gold/black cover in between).

Both the Quarter Jack and the astronomical clock are driven by mechanisms kept in the bell tower above them. When it comes to timekeeping, this place certainly doesn't do things by halves. It does them by quarters.

Address Wimborne Minster, High Street, Wimborne BH21 1EB, +44 (0)1202 884753, www.wimborneminster.org.uk, parishoffice@wimborneminster.org.uk | Getting there By car, take A350, A349 and B3073; bus 3 or 4 towards Wimborne Minster, to The Square | Tip Inside the Minster, there's the tomb of King Ethelred, brother of Alfred the Great (you know, the one with all the burnt cakes).

75 RNLI Training Pool
In at the deep end

Feeling thirsty? At 25 metres long, 12 metres wide and 4 metres deep, if you were to drink this sea-survival training pool dry, it would take you 1,260 years at five pints a day. *Gulp!* This is the largest survival training pool in the UK and is housed inside the Royal National Lifeboat Institution (RNLI) Training College. Crew from all over the country come here to receive training on sea rescues. Five different wave motions – some as high as 1.4 metres – can be simulated in the pool, along with staged thunder, lightning, wind, rain and total darkness. Before the team enter the water via the 'jump platform', they are given 23 seconds to change into their survival suits – a red wetsuit-type get-up resembling one of the Teletubbies. Once submerged, they go about their training, which includes abandoning ship and how to deal with a capsized boat.

As well as brewing up storms for RNLI volunteers, this pool has also been used in the making of TV programmes like *Blue Peter*, corporate videos, adverts and trailers. In 2008, Paramount Comedy filmed an advertising campaign here for the American sitcom *Two and a Half Men*. The BBC and Discovery Channel have also got in on the 'lights, camera, action' to create realistic sea conditions for their programmes.

The RNLI offers College Discovery Tours, which show you around its training facilities, including this impressive pool and the lifeboat simulator, which replicates a perilous scenario at sea, with much rocking, wave-crashing and stormy weather. Warning: skip this part if you get seasick. *Bleugh!*

This amazing charity has saved more than 140,000 lives since it began in 1824. In 2016, its volunteer lifeboat crews rescued 8,851 people and saved 431 lives. Its motto comes from its founder Sir William Hillary: 'With courage, nothing is impossible'. Nothing… except, maybe, drinking the entire contents of the training pool.

Address West Quay Road, BH15 1HZ, +44 (0)300 300 7654, www.rnli.org/rnli-college, reception@rnli.org.uk | Getting there 10-minute walk from Poole Bus Station: take Lifeboat Quay, Holes Bay Road and West Quay Road. It's next to Asda. | Hours The 90-minute College Discovery Tours take place daily Mon–Thu 11am and/or 2.30pm, Fri 3pm, Sat 11am (subject to volunteer availability – call to check times) | Tip The other tour on offer is the All-weather Lifeboat Centre (ALC) Tour, where you'll see how the RNLI's lifeboats are built, refitted, repaired and maintained in the factory.

76 Radar Memorial
Not flying in under the radar

Microwaves: making leftovers a viable dinner option since 1946. Had it not been for the work carried out during World War II in Worth Matravers, you might have been destined to eat cold spag Bol the day after you made a batch. You might also be speaking German. You see, between May 1940 and May 1942, Worth Matravers was at the centre of radar development in the UK, which was crucial to the winning of the war. The top-secret work also paved the way for the technology used in telephone, TV and satellite communications, air traffic control, LCD (liquid crystal display) monitors, speed cameras, medical body scanners and – *hurrah!* – microwave ovens.

This stainless-steel memorial, perched on the clifftop at St Aldhelm's Head, commemorates the pioneering research carried out here. It represents two radar dishes, arranged in such a way that they also form (no, not a fruit bowl) a large fire basket. As such, both old and modern methods to warn of invasion are signified – fires were lit as beacons to warn of impending attack; radar is the modern equivalent. During World War II, radar was used to detect approaching hostile aircraft, which could then be intercepted by British fighter planes. Radar was also fitted inside aircraft, which helped bombers to locate enemy ships and surfaced submarines.

The local sculptor Tony Viney crafted the memorial, which was unveiled on 27 October, 2001, by Sir Bernard Lovell, one of the 2,000 radar researchers at Worth Matravers. His wartime colleague, Dr Bill Penley, was also at the unveiling. Penley died in 2017 in Poole Hospital at the age of 99 years and 10 months.

After a hard day's radar-ing, such scientists would frequent the Square & Compass pub (ch. 87), which they nicknamed – nerd alert! – 'Sine & Cosine' after the mathematical terms they used in their research. We've got these guys to thank for our reheated food, and for our freedom.

Address St Aldhelm's Head, Worth Matravers, Swanage BH19 3LN | Getting there By car, A350, A35, A351 and B3069, through Worth Matravers, park at Renscombe Car Park and walk 1.5 miles by following the sign to St Aldhelm's (the memorial is only accessible on foot) | Tip Next to the memorial is the National Coastwatch Institution (NCI) tower, manned by volunteers to be the 'eyes and ears along the coast', watching out for anyone on the sea in distress. It's open to the public and they have some literature about the 'radar days'.

77 River Piddle
Flowing through the silver screen

Looking at the modest River Piddle, you'd never guess that it once posed as the deepest river in the world: the Congo River. And yet, in the 1951 Oscar-winning film *The African Queen*, this is just what it did. The filmmakers cleverly used the river mouth to film the boat pushing through the reeds. Filmgoers had no idea that they weren't watching Africa on the big screen. The scene where the German U-boat is spotted was shot where the Hamworthy Marine Camp now sits, and a Parkstone fisherman's boat was used as another German craft. Throughout filming, the stars of the film, Humphrey Bogart and Katharine Hepburn, are said to have stayed in the Black Bear Hotel in Wareham, where they would drink at the public bar.

The River Piddle flows south and then south-east, almost parallel to the larger River Frome, to Wareham, where they both enter Poole Harbour via Wareham Channel. The river's name has had a number of spellings over the years. In 966 AD it was called the Pidelen, then the Pydel. It runs through several villages, and many are named after it, with the names being derived from variants of 'piddle' or 'puddle'. Tolpuddle is famous as the home of the Tolpuddle Martyrs, who were sentenced to penal transportation to Australia after they created a friendly society – or trade union of sorts – in 1833. After the river became the Piddle, Queen Victoria was due to visit the area as a young girl, and locals changed the name to Puddle, concerned that Piddle was offensive. Today, it remains River Piddle.

The English novelist Thomas Hardy took inspiration from the river and the surrounding villages. The All Saints' Church graveyard in Piddletrenthide contains two headstones marking the graves of members of the Dumberfeild family. A plaque, standing slightly askew, reads: 'Members of the family immortalised by Thomas Hardy in *Tess of the D'Urbervilles*.'

Address Wareham | Getting there A350, A35, A351, at Saxon Roundabout take the first exit | Tip You can drink a pint of Piddle (which is more pleasant than it sounds). Piddle Brewery crafts an array of beers and ciders beside the River Piddle. Among others, they produce Piddle Premium Ale, Martyrs' Relief Best Bitter and Dorset Rogue Best Bitter (www.piddlebrewery.co.uk).

78 Sandbanks Carved Rocks
Making a fist of things

Like the Easter Island statues, the Pyramids and Stonehenge, the carved rocks resting among the other 'normal' rocks outside the Haven Hotel at Sandbanks are shrouded in mystery. How did they get there? Who crafted them? And why? Could it be the case that 'Sandbanksy' has struck? The giant 'Hand of the Harbour' comes complete with knuckles, veins and a huge thumbnail. The sculptor certainly went to town on the details, making it likely that passersby will imagine the BFG is clinging to the rock, about to clamber to the surface. The 'Faces by the Ferry' are similarly intricate, with one resembling a freaky gargoyle and another sporting a crown of sorts.

Poole locals have a few theories as to the origins of these befuddling boulders, which appeared in the late 1990s. One is that they are scrapped carvings from a nearby quarry (discarded by the artist who wasn't satisfied with their handiwork) that made their way here along with the other boulders being used for sea defence. It's a plausible explanation. Another suggestion is that they hail from the lost city of Atlantis. Less plausible. The style of the carvings is similar to that of local sculptor Jonathan Sells, who created the Wareham Market Statue (ch. 102), and many people have asked him over the years if he's the phantom chiseller. He's not.

If you're interested to see more stone carvings, head to Tout Quarry Sculpture Park in Portland, the southernmost point of Dorset. There you'll also find a few faces and a hand, although this one is much smaller and more of a child-sized imprint. Work your way around the map, which outlines 54 sculptures, including an octopus, a whale's tail, a bear's head and a fireplace.

Someone *must* know how the carved rocks at Sandbanks came to be. But they're certainly not making it common knowledge. And why should they? Nothing beats a good mystery.

Address Sandbanks BH13 7QL | Getting there Bus Breezer 60 towards Sandbanks to Ferry Approach. Climb down the metal ladder on the left side of the car park (if you're looking at the sea) by the chain ferry. | Tip Feeling inspired? Grab a chisel and book onto one of Jonathan Sells' stone-carving lessons (www.jonathan-sells.com/stone-carving-teaching).

79 _ Sculpture by the Lakes
Namaste: now I'm gonna stay

Turn off your phone, ignore your groaning to-do list, and forget about checking social media for a few hours. It's time to get your Zen on at Sculpture by the Lakes, where the biggest decision you'll have to make is whether to turn left or right at the *Bird of Happiness*. Set in 26 acres of splendid countryside, this sculpture park is the biggest art gallery in Dorset, without the constraints of a traditional gallery – like walls.

Wander the paths and take in the 34 (mostly bronze) sculptures nestled in nature as you hear the birds tweeting, the leaves rustling and the River Frome flowing. The sculptor, Simon Gudgeon, is inspired by birds – with swans, falcons, owls, pelicans, cranes, and 'The Raven' from Edgar Allan Poe's poem featuring in his captivating collection. A quote about birds also features, with his *Sphere* sculpture citing the words of American author Henry van Dyke: 'Use what talents you possess: the woods would be very silent if no birds sang there except those that sang best.' A heads-up: you'll likely get dizzy when reading this.

It's not just birds that get Gudgeon's creative juices flowing. One of the more striking sculptures in the park is *Search for Enlightenment* – two huge heads with gaping holes. The seed of the idea for this piece came when he stood atop an African mountain watching the sun set, while musing on 'the transience of humanity'. If this piece moves you, one of the five limited-edition models could be yours for a cool £295,000. Or why not sit on the 'IDEAS' bench and hope that your artistic genius strikes? If not, it's still a lovely spot for a sandwich and a sit down.

This oasis of tranquillity is the perfect backdrop to the meditation retreats (run by an actual Buddhist monk), yoga retreats, tai chi qigong shibashi instruction, wellbeing festivals, art workshops and sound healing baths that occur here. Aaaaand reeeelaaax.

Address Pallington Lakes, Dorchester DT2 8QU, +44 (0)7720 637808, www.sculpturebythelakes.co.uk, office@sculpturebythelakes.co.uk | **Getting there** By car, A350, A35 | **Hours** 1 Apr–30 Sep Wed–Sun, 1 Oct–30 Mar Tue–Sat, 10am–5pm | **Tip** Pop into the Gallery, where you can browse and buy smaller versions of the outside sculptures, as well as pieces from other artists.

80 Shillingstone Station

Fit for a king... and a puppet

From Prince Charles getting his shoelaces ironed to the Queen's corgis having their own chef, the Royals are no strangers to being treated with higher regard than the rest of us. A reminder of this is at Shillingstone Railway Station. The ornate canopy was erected in 1903 for frequent visitor the Prince of Wales, later King Edward VII, who'd alight here when staying with the noble residents of Iwerne Minster House (now Clayesmore School).

Just as it was offered to the king, a warm welcome greets all who visit Shillingstone Station's cafe, museum and shop today. In 2016, it even welcomed a production of Noël Coward's *Still Life*, which was performed inside the restored 1957 carriage on the tracks. Shillingstone is the last remaining station of the Dorset Central Railway (which later became part of the Somerset and Dorset Joint Railway). During Operation Pied Piper in World War II, the platforms were bustling with children evacuated from the cities. It also had a hand in Operation Overlord (ch. 62), which almost got cancelled when vital supplies failed to reach Blandford Camp. Guess where the missing wagon was discovered. Shillingstone! The station also has a claim to fame in the shape of glove puppet Sooty. He 'lived' in nearby village Child Okeford with his puppeteer Harry Corbett and, in the 1950s, children would flock from Bournemouth to Shillingstone to attend Sooty's garden parties.

Having opened on 31 August, 1863, the station closed on 7 March, 1966, as a result of cutbacks. In 2006, the Shillingstone Railway Project (now operated by the North Dorset Railway Trust) began restoration work to bring it back to life. Tracks were re-laid, the garden was replanted and many wagons, locomotives and carriages were bought and restored. The long-term goal is to get a steam train back up and chugging along the tracks, to offer rides to Sturminster Newton and back. *Choo choo!*

Address St. Parick's Industrial Estate, Shillingstone, Blandford Forum DT11 0SA, +44 (0)1258 860696, www.shillingstone-railway-project.org.uk, info@shillingstone-railway-project.org.uk | **Getting there** By car, A350, A354 and A350, at Badger Roundabout take third exit onto A354, at Hill Top Roundabout continue straight onto A350, left onto A357, right onto Station Road | **Hours** Wed, Sat & Sun 10am–4pm | **Tip** In World War I, Shillingstone was named the 'bravest village in Britain' due to the high proportion of residents who volunteered to join the Armed Forces. Perhaps fittingly, the lyrics for the hymn 'Onward Christian Soldiers' were composed in Hanford, just five minutes up the road.

81 __ Shitterton

A most excrement adventure

The hamlet of Shitterton has received worldwide attention due to its crude – and, yes, amusing – name. It was voted 'Britain's Worst Place Name' in 2012. A couple of years prior, the villagers grew so irked by the area's entrance sign continually being stolen (the ultimate beer trophy?) that they had a whip-round to pay for an immovable Purbeck-stone one, set in concrete. It cost them £680 and weighs 1.5 tonnes. Eat shit, thieves!

The name Shitterton dates back at least 1,000 years to the Anglo-Saxon period, being recorded in the Domesday Book in Norman French as 'Scatera' or 'Scetra', which have derivations from the word 'dung'. The name gives a nod to the stream that crosses the hamlet, which was called the 'Shiter' or 'Shitter', meaning 'brook used as a privy'. Shitterton, therefore, has been translated to mean 'farmstead on the stream used as an open sewer'. Anyone got a nose peg? But, these days, the hamlet and stream are a lot more charming than their names suggest. Indeed, the only 'poo' you'll see floating down the stream now is from a game of Poohsticks that you might play from the picturesque bridge. And rather than having crappy names, the thatched homes sound positively adorable – with Dairy Cottage, Mulberry View and Bluebell Cottage being among them, and free-range eggs often being sold outside. Oh, and the mischievously named Pooh Corner (fnar fnar) at number 13 shows that Shitter-tonites have a sense of humour.

Shitterton has had a variety of spellings throughout its existence: 'Schitereston' in 1285; 'Shyterton' in 1332; 'Chiterton' in 1456; and 'Shetterton' in 1687. In the 19th century, Victorians tried to refine the name Shitterton by losing the 'h' to make it Sitterton. Nice try, but over the years it reverted back to its more memorable name (as did the nearby River Piddle, ch. 77), although Sitterton Close and Sitterton House defiantly remain.

Address Bere Regis, Wareham BH20 7HU | Getting there By car, follow A350 and A35 to Poole Hill in Bere Regis, then take West Street to Shitterton | Tip For more titter-inducing place names nearby, visit Happy Bottom in Corfe Mullen, Knacker's Hole in Sturminster Newton, or Dungy Head, Scratchy Bottom and Shaggs – all near Lulworth.

82__ The Silent Woman Inn
A speakeasy this ain't

They say silence is golden, but in the case of this public house, silence is positively barbaric. Once a smugglers' hangout, legend has it that the loose-tongued, verbose landlady let slip the smugglers' secrets in Wareham marketplace: *'You'll never guess where all that gin's buried... Ships of the stuff... Wouldn't mind some of that lace myself...'* Terrified of being captured by the dreaded excisemen, the smugglers turned all 'gangster' and savagely cut out her tongue, thus creating the silent (and probably rather peeved) woman.

Three people (men) who weren't silent when frequenting this pub were Prime Minister Winston Churchill, General Dwight D. Eisenhower and General Bernard Montgomery, who would meet here in 1944, in the run-up to D-Day, to discuss tactics (ch. 30). Bovington Camp, the British Army military base, is about 10 miles away from the Silent Woman Inn, and when Princes William and Harry were training there, they would pop in. On one occasion, William caused quite a stir when he drove a tank into the car park, churning up much of the grass in the process. The previous landlord, Richard Bell, came out remonstrating, until he saw who the culprit was, which is when he bit his tongue (lucky for him, he still had one to bite). Prince William was profusely apologetic and returned the next day to fix the damage. For years, a caricature of the whole scene hung on a wall inside the pub, but it was removed when the property changed hands in 2020.

On the outside of the building is the image of a decapitated woman carrying her own head in her hands, with the words *Since the woman is quiet let no man breed a rio*t underneath. You wouldn't read about it! Well, actually, you would. In Thomas Hardy's 1878 novel *Return of the Native*, the same gruesome figure and rhyme appear in the sign for his fictional pub The Quiet Woman. A tongue-in-cheek acknowledgement of the controversial book if ever there was one.

Address Bere Road, Coldharbour, Wareham BH20 7PA, +44 (0)1929 552909,
www.thesilentwoman.co.uk, info@thesilentwoman.co.uk | Getting there By car, A350,
A35, A351 to Bere Road | Hours Opening hours vary throughout the year – see website
for details | Tip Wareham Forest is very nearby and a lovely place for a walk or cycle.

83 _ Sir Peter Thompson House

Carry on nurse

If you're in Poole and require a blood test, have a broken leg or need an X-ray, you'll go to Poole Hospital on Longfleet Road. If, however, you required medical assistance between 1897 and 1907, you'd have gone to Sir Peter Thompson House. Not that the merchant, antiquary and MP knew anything about this: he died in 1770. Established by philanthropist and all-round 'good egg' Lady Cornelia Spencer-Churchill (known as Lady Wimborne after marrying Ivor Bertie Guest, the 1st Baron Wimborne), Cornelia Hospital was set up inside the mansion house, originally built as a retirement home for Thompson in 1746. Its large rooms were converted into wards that contained a total of 18 beds. The matron, Harriet Raven (who played a vital role in setting the hospital up), two nurses, a housemaid, a cook and a porter all lived on-site to tend to the patients.

Lady Cornelia founded three hospitals in Poole. Prior to the one at Sir Peter Thompson House, she had first set up the Cornelia Cottage Hospital on West Street in 1889. It was divided into three wards: male, female and convalescent. After the hospital at Sir Peter Thompson House closed in 1907, it was relocated to its current position on Longfleet Road (previously Ringwood Road) to allow space for future expansion. It cost around £3,400 to construct and held 14 beds. During World War I, it was forced to improvise – the waiting room being transformed into a makeshift ward with beds donated by locals – as an influx of wounded soldiers arrived. Throughout the war, Cornelia Hospital treated 2,583 military patients, whilst still caring for locals. It was renamed Poole General Hospital in 1948, then demolished and rebuilt – at a cost of £5 million – by July 1969, when an opening ceremony was attended by Queen Elizabeth II. Poole Hospital now has 789 beds, as well as the Cornelia Suite on the fifth floor, which offers private patients rooms with a view of Poole Harbour. Lady Cornelia's legacy lives on.

Address 25 Market Close, BH15 1NE | Getting there A three-minute walk from Poole High Street; a six-minute walk from Poole Quay | Tip Lady Cornelia has certainly left her mark locally: there's a Cornelia Crescent, Cornelia Gardens, Cornelia Lodge, Cornelia House and Cornelia Road.

84 Skerryvore

Where a literary genius blew raspberries

As you step into the commemorative garden of Skerryvore, home of *Dr Jekyll and Mr Hyde* author Robert Louis Stevenson, try to imagine this domestic scene: his wife Fanny, a keen gardener, tending to the fruits of her labour – apples, pears, plums, raspberries, tomatoes and Indian corn – while her husband sits in the sunshine, with a rough wooden board on his knee, writing. Such scenes, along with an account of Stevenson unwittingly hacking his wife's raspberry bushes to bits (as a gardener he made a great writer), are found in the 1926 *R.L.S. and His Sine Qua Non: Flashlights from Skerryvore by The Gamekeeper* by Adelaide Boodle.

Stevenson – ranked the 26th most translated author in the world – lived at Skerryvore between April 1885 and August 1887 in the hope that the sea air would help his chronic bronchial illness. It was during this time that he penned, among others, his most famous work, *Strange Case of Dr Jekyll and Mr Hyde*, the chilling idea for which came to him in a dream. He named the character of Mr Poole, Dr Jekyll's butler, after the town of Poole. This gothic novella sold 40,000 copies in Britain in the first six months of publication, but Stevenson threw the first draft in the fire after his wife's criticism that it was no allegorical masterpiece. Well, you know what they say: behind every successful man stands a woman with a fire stoker.

Stevenson was Scottish, and named his house Skerryvore after the tallest lighthouse in Scotland, which had been built by his Uncle Alan. The only structure that stands on the plot today (sadly, the house was bombed in a German air raid in 1940, and demolished in the 1950s) is a mini replica of this lighthouse. During spring, it is flanked by scads of wild snowdrops and bluebells – as is the rest of the garden – in a chaotically beautiful manner. Much like, one would imagine, the inside of Stevenson's creative mind.

85 — Slop Bog
A phizz-whizzer of a nature reserve

Although it may sound like a location straight out of a Roald Dahl book, you're unlikely to see the BFG, any Oompa-Loompas or, indeed, Bruce Bogtrotter wandering about the 56 acres of this local nature reserve. You will, however, see a glut of wildlife. Amongst your garden-variety woodland dwellers, you may also spot some rarer members of the critter kingdom, such as the silver-studded blue butterfly (which, in the summer, flutter around in a mating frenzy), the Dartford warbler bird (which almost became extinct in the UK in the last century), the red damselfly (not to be mistaken with a dragonfly, of which Slop Bog is home to at least 11 species), and the adder (the UK's only poisonous snake – yikes!).

There are also around 70 species of fungi lurking in the woods. With names like Poison Pie, Stinking Parasol, False Death Cap and The Deceiver, perhaps it's best you don't go foraging for mushrooms for your dinner here.

Slop Bog has been under threat for many years. In 1759, it was part of the old Hampreston Heath, which stretched from the New Forest to the Purbecks but, by 1985, it had gradually been whittled down to its current size by housing developments, roads and the like. The Stewart family used Slop Bog to grow pond plants – particularly waterlilies – to sell via the first ever mail-order plant catalogue. In 1955, they opened Stewarts in Ferndown, the first garden centre in the UK, which is still there today.

You can't visit this Site of Special Scientific Interest (SSSI) without taking a stroll over the boardwalk, which allows visitors to cross the sphagnum bog without the need for wellies. You could give pond-dipping a bash to see what creatures you might catch. If you're lucky, you could net a raft spider, a pond skater or a whirligig beetle. Or perhaps even a palmate newt that would have *Matilda*'s Miss Trunchbull quaking in her boots.

Address 33 Hazel Drive, Ferndown BH22 9SP (note that this postcode won't get you to the entrances if using a satnav), www.slopbog.org | **Getting there** There are three entrances to Slop Bog: on Cedar Way, on Redwood Drive and near West Moors Road (the entrance is on the right side of the main road). For detailed instructions on how to get there, visit www.slopbog.org/location. Only on-street parking is available. | **Tip** Grab a cake and a coffee at the Broomhill Stewarts Garden Centre. Pick up some shrubs and perennials while you're there, too (www.stewarts.co.uk).

86 SoundCellar

All that jazz

Writer John O'Farrell once said, 'Music is a journey. Jazz is getting lost.' If you feel like getting lost, head to SoundCellar, a jazz night held fortnightly at The Blue Boar pub. Its intimate, exposed-brick-cool setting provides the perfect ambience and acoustics for riffs, licks and chords galore. SoundCellar began in 2009, set up by jazz lover and guitarist Rob Palmer. It's become a well-known venue on the jazz-music scene and is Poole's answer to Ronnie Scott's. It has hosted a huge array of talented artists, including Sting's keyboard player Jason Rebello, Pink Floyd's saxophonist Gilad Atzmon, Sheryl Crow's drummer Jeremy Stacey, and Oasis' guitarist/keyboard player Paul Stacey. There are usually around 35 people in the audience, but on the night that Becca Stevens – who has collaborated with Grammy-award-winning jazz ensemble Snarky Puppy – performed, the place was bursting at the seams with 90 fans tapping their feet, clapping their hands and rhythmically patting their thighs.

Among the crazy-talented people to have taken to the SoundCellar stage is drummer Paul Clarvis. Having worked with some of the music greats, including Mick Jagger, Paul McCartney, Elton John, Nina Simone, Stevie Wonder and Bryan Ferry, he's also played for dozens of movie soundtracks, including *Lord of the Rings*, *Star Wars*, *Harry Potter* and *James Bond*. Oh, and *Kung Fu Panda*. He also led the biggest troupe of drummers ever assembled in the UK for the thrilling 2012 Olympics opening ceremony in London.

It's taken a while but SoundCellar is finally registering on the wider world's radar. In July 2019, the gig played there led by saxophonist Tony Woods was recorded for BBC Radio 3's *Jazz Now* show. A SoundCellar gig will take you on a jazz journey, navigating grooves, blues and tap-my-shoes. You may lose yourself but, if the music speaks to you, you may also find yourself.

Address The Blue Boar, 29 Market Close, BH15 1NE, www.soundcellar.org, soundcellarmusic@yahoo.co.uk | Getting there Five-minute walk from Poole Quay, seven-minute walk from Poole Bus Station | Hours Usually Thursday evenings fortnightly (check website for specific gigs) | Tip Want more jazz? Check out the annual Swanage Jazz Festival (swanagejazzfestival.co.uk).

87 Square & Compass

A pub you can really dig

You know some pubs are a bit samey, a bit… meh? This isn't one of them. Square & Compass has personality in spades. Let's start with its museum of fossils, oddities and local finds. As well as the Jurassic Coast fossils, ammonites and bones, there's also archaeological gems such as Roman jewellery, 18th-century shipwreck treasures like silver pieces of eight, sharks' teeth, a stuffed fox, a turtle shell, and… what's that? Cripes! It's the skull of a ram! The pub's landlord, Charlie Newman, opened this museum in 1998 in memory of his father, also an avid, and well-respected, fossil hunter. His finds in Swanage Bay were so important, in fact, that in the 1960s they were catalogued by the National History Museum. And when it came to making a name for himself in the palaeontology world, like father like son: when researchers discovered fossils of what may be our oldest mammalian ancestor, on the Durlston cliffs, they named it 'Durlstotherium newmani' after Charlie Newman, who helped collect the specimens.

When Charlie's not unearthing history, he's making cider – about 24,000 litres a year – which is sold from a hatch (there's no bar counter) in the Square & Compass, as is no-fuss food like pasties, sausage rolls and pies, served on paper plates. Originally built in the 18th century as a pair of cottages, the pub has been in the Newman family since 1907. It was given its name in 1830 by then-landlord Charles Bower, who was a stonemason. Squares and compasses were the tools used in such a profession, and a giant wooden structure of them can be found in the garden, along with the resident chickens and a stunning sea view.

As well as the live music that's regularly played here, there are a number of kooky annual events, including the Fossil Fayre, Stone Carving Festival, Hobby Horse Dressage & Jumping, and the Beard, Bottled Beer & Cheese Festival. Be there or be square.

Address Worth Matravers, Swanage BH19 3LF, +44 (0)1929 439229,
www.squareandcompasspub.co.uk, kevin@squareandcompasspub.co.uk | Getting there By
car, A35, A351 and B3069; bus Breezer 40 to Haycrafts Lane, then a 1.4-mile walk | Hours
Daily noon–11pm | Tip In a field near the pub, the landlord constructed a tree-trunk
sculpture called *Woodhenge*. It's 10 metres wide, 3.5 metres high and weighs about 35 tonnes.

88 St Aldhelm's Chapel
You wish

When you drop a penny into a wishing well, what do you wish for? To win the lottery? For a promotion? To have firmer abs? If you'd frequented St Aldhelm's Chapel in the 17th century, you might have dropped a pin or hairpin into one of the holes in its central pillar and wished to find love. At this time, the chapel was no longer used for worship, so young girls would pop into this 'wishing chapel' in a bid to guide Cupid's aim towards the man of their dreams.

It was around this time that the earliest graffiti was gouged into the pillar. Crosses, names, initials and dates (ranging from the 1600s to the 1950s) have all been carved here. See if you can find Augusta Grant's engraving – her beautiful cursive script is rather impressive. Those defacing this pillar may have had to jostle some visiting cows, though. These bovine intruders got to be a problem, so a gate and fence were constructed outside the door of the chapel in order to keep them out. By July 1963, however, Daisy and her crew had got the message that they weren't welcome; the barriers were removed, no longer required.

This 12th-century Norman building contains several architectural features that are unusual for a chapel. Firstly, its shape. The 7.77-metre-long walls meet to make a square, with each corner orientated towards the cardinal points of a compass. The lack of altar suggests it might not initially have been built as a place of worship, but rather as a watchtower for Corfe Castle, which remained incomplete. It's also been suggested that it was a navigation aid for passing ships (with a beacon on top where the cross now sits), having been described in 1625 as a 'sea-marke'.

Today, however, it is most definitely a chapel. Special services are held throughout the year, as well as evening services in August. It's also used for wedding ceremonies, so perhaps the pins in the pillar are still working their romantic magic.

Address St Aldhelm's Head, Worth Matravers, Swanage BH19 3LN | Getting there By car, A350, A35, A351 and B3069, through Worth Matravers, park at Renscombe Car Park and walk 1.5 miles to the chapel by following the sign to St Aldhelm's (the chapel is only accessible on foot) | Hours Chapel is open 24/7 (door only closed, never locked, during seriously inclement weather) | Tip It's not obvious at first but look closer and you'll see that the chapel is built within a series of earthworks, which probably surrounded a Christian enclosure prior to the Norman Conquest.

89 St James' Weathervane

A catch in the wind

'Dear God, let the fish be plentiful and the sea be kind. Amen'. This prayer, or a variation of it, has probably been uttered countless times inside the walls of St James' Church (which has appeared on BBC's *Songs of Praise*). The church, first built in 1142, then rebuilt in 1819, is located near Poole Quay and has long been associated with the local fishing trade, earning itself the nickname 'The Fisherman's Church'. Hence the unusual fish-shaped weathervane on top of the building. The spikes on the fish's back don't indicate what type it is; instead, they were likely added to stop seagulls from landing on it. Another local church with a fish weathervane is Christchurch Priory, alluding to the fact that Christchurch was once renowned for its salmon.

Another nod to marine life at St James' Church is the scallop shell, which is the symbol of St James, one of the 12 apostles of Jesus. Three scallop shells – or St James' cockles – are on Poole's coat of arms (along with a dolphin), which can be seen inside the church in the north gallery. A couple of the stained-glass windows also run (or swim) with the sea/fish theme. The 1957 Goff Memorial Window depicts Jesus, his disciples and a fishing boat, while the 1999 Tilsed Memorial Window shows a net enveloping 153 fish during 'the miraculous catch of fish'.

If it weren't for fish, the pipe organ might never have ended up here in 1799. It was a gift from Benjamin Lester, a Poole merchant who made oceans of cash from the salt-cod trade with Newfoundland (ch. 39). It was from Trinity in Newfoundland that the pine columns supporting the vaulted roof inside the church were brought over on sailing brigs in 1820.

The sea and its inhabitants play a significant role in the character and spirit of St James' Church. Seeing as the fish is a symbol of Christianity, what could be more fitting?

Address Church Street, BH15 1JP, +44 (0)1202 677117, www.stjameschurchpoole.weebly.com | Getting there Five-minute walk from Poole Quay | Hours The church can usually be accessed Tue–Fri 9.30am–1pm | Tip Fancy your own fish weathervane? Dorset Weathervanes has a whole school of them for sale (www.weathervanes-direct.co.uk).

90 Studland Bay

Are the seahorses riding towards extinction?

Besides being home to the most popular naturist beach in Britain, Studland Bay is also the most important site for seahorses in the British Isles. The biggest seahorse ever found in the wild was caught in Poole Harbour by a local fisherman in 2015. After measuring it at 34 cm long, he threw it back into the sea. If he'd have kept it, he'd have faced legal action – both the spiny and short-snouted species of seahorses (Studland Bay is the only site in the UK where both these species breed) are protected under the Wildlife and Countryside Act 1981, which prevents them from being killed, injured or taken. These fragile creatures' numbers are dwindling: in 2008, around 40 seahorses were recorded in Studland Bay, but in 2017, there were only 14. None were spotted for nearly three years between 2015 and 2017. The first seahorse to be seen in the Studland area after all that time was given the name Hope. During 2020's COVID-19 lockdown, the seahorse population began to thrive again due to less people and fewer boats in the area, but this boost in numbers was short-lived.

Studland also has a host of other marine life in residence, including the endangered undulate ray. In 2015, there was much excitement among the marine biology community when these billowing beauties were caught on camera gliding through the eel grass in Studland Bay. Such is their colouring and markings – which have been likened to Aboriginal art – that they are all but camouflaged so can be very hard to spot. In the autumn and winter months, hundreds of undulate ray egg cases (charmingly known as mermaids' purses) can be found along the four-mile stretch of the golden, sandy beach of Studland Bay.

This beach – on a different note – is the setting for Coldplay's *Yellow* music video, which sees Chris Martin walking in slow-motion along the shore. Luckily, Mr Martin didn't trip over any of these mermaids' purses – or encounter any nudists – so the video was achieved in one continuous shot, with no cuts.

Address Ferry Road, Studland BH19 3AQ | Getting there Bus 50 to Heathland House or Beach Road; pay-and-display car parks at South Beach, Middle Beach, Knoll Beach and Shell Bay; chain ferry from Sandbanks to Studland Bay for both foot passengers and vehicles | Tip Shell Bay Restaurant & Bistro, on the right as you come off the ferry, has stunning views of Brownsea Island, Poole Harbour and Sandbanks. Sit in the restaurant (civilised, like) or chill in one of the hammocks on the deck. Swaying with a sun-downer optional, but highly recommended (shellbay.net).

91 Sunseeker International
Splashing the cash

From canoes to catamarans, powerboats to pedalos, Poole is teeming with boats. But none is more impressive than the Sunseeker superyacht. Oozing luxurious glamour, Sunseekers are synonymous with the fabulous, famous and filthy rich – John Travolta, Michael Douglas, Simon Cowell and Jenson Button are all customers. Sunseeker International – previously Poole Powerboats – has its headquarters and main assembly point in Poole. It was founded by Robert Braithwaite in 1969 and now exports around 150 yachts a year to more than 74 countries. The largest and most technologically advanced boat the company has ever produced is the Sunseeker 155 Yacht, which costs around £20 million (bikini-clad models dancing on the deck not included).

If your budget is more kayak than ker-ching, more dinghy than dollars, you can live vicariously through characters on the big screen. *Absolutely Fabulous: The Movie* sees Edina and Patsy quaffing champagne – dahling! – on the Sunseeker motor yacht *Thumper* while cruising around the coast of Cannes. The 2017 *Logan* mentions Sunseeker no less than five times, with Hugh Jackman's character trying to purchase a 1996 Sunseeker for $60K – cash. But it's James Bond who simply can't get enough of the super-slick Sunseeker. Various 'seekers have appeared in four consecutive Bond films – *The World is Not Enough* in 1999, *Die Another Day* in 2002, *Casino Royale* in 2006 and *Quantum of Solace* in 2008. It was in *Quantum of Solace* that Braithwaite featured in a cameo role as a speedboat captain. When he was alive, even though he lived in the brash world of the uber-rich, he was generous. When the land next to the RNLI (ch. 75) went up for sale, he withdrew Sunseeker's offer, saying that the RNLI's need was greater. He also gifted a £3.5-million surgical robot to Poole Hospital. After all, when it comes to health and humanity, we're all in the same boat.

Address 7 The Quay, BH15 1HA, +44 (0)1202 666060, www.sunseeker.com, info@sunseeker.com | Getting there 14-minute walk from Poole Bus Station | Tip Once you've had your fill of drooling over the multimillion-pound Sunseekers, walk along Poole Quay and board a pleasure cruise, an altogether more affordable option (www.citycruisespoole.com).

92 Swanage Old Gaol

From one slammer to the next

Measuring just 5½ feet by 7 feet, there's not enough room to swing a cat in this little lock-up, let alone do the 'Jailhouse Rock' or the 'Cell Block Tango'. But, likely used most frequently as a temporary drunk tank for the rowdy residents of Swanage in the 19th century, it's probably heard its fair share of out-of-tune singing. Constructed in 1803, the sign above the door reads: *Erected For the Prevention of Vice & Immorality By The Friends of Religion & good Order.* The rectangular, gabled, stone building has a nail-studded door and a single window covered with a grille (perhaps if people came to taunt offenders through the window, they'd slur in response: 'Oi, get outta my grille!').

The 'Friends of Religion & good Order' might have also deemed it necessary to lock up 'ladies of the night', similar to the likes of Cockle Kate. Cockle Kate was the nickname given to infamous Poole prostitute and drunkard Kate Elizabeth Cartridge. In the 1900s, this short, plump brunette became popular with sailors (and not just because she swore like one) and dockers, and unpopular with most everyone else, particularly pub landlords who frequently had to throw her out for being a nuisance, and her son's teacher who was left scratched and bleeding following a run-in with her. Cockle Kate had a colourful reputation; she was loud, obnoxious and no stranger to the law, being convicted of being drunk and disorderly on 21 March, 1907. She was sentenced to 14 days' hard labour and declared a Habitual Drunkard, which meant it was illegal for her to purchase any more alcohol.

Swanage Old Gaol would have been a terribly claustrophobic place to be detained. Inside, it has a circular dished setting. Historians suggest it was for washing but, based on who would have been spending the night there, perhaps it's the 19th-century equivalent of a bucket by the bed.

Erected
For the Prevention
of
Vice & Immorality
By
The Friends of Religion & good Order
A.D.1803.

Address Swanage BH19 2NZ | **Getting there** By car, A350, A35 and A351 to High Street in Swanage; bus Breezer 30, Breezer 40 or Breezer 50 to Swanage Bus Station. The Old Gaol is down a small path to the right of Swanage Town Hall. | **Tip** Urban Health & Fitness on Christchurch Road used to be the Swinging Clink nightclub in the 1960s and 1970s. It was decorated like a prison and the owner would cycle round town dressed as a convict to promote the place.

93 Swanage Pier

Take a walk on the mild side

Got your dosh. Bollocks to you matey... 40 pigs ate the wood... Rat Bag loves Grot Bag... Stroll along Swanage Pier and, amongst the 11,000-plus brass plaques you'll walk over, as well as the 'in loving memory' and 'happy birthday' ones, you'll also find these 'in-jokes'. You'll see a couple of marriage proposals, as well – it's rather lovely that on the spot where a couple's future begins, they're standing on something with such a rich history.

Prior to this Victorian pier being built, there was another pier in Swanage, constructed in 1859/60 and primarily used for shipping Purbeck stone. Up to 50,000 tonnes of stone were stored on the seafront, where The Parade is now. In 1874, with a constant stream of day-trippers onto the pier, it became clear that an 'overflow pier' was required – not least to save the women's hems and shoes from all the dust and mayhem.

On 29 March, 1897 – *fanfare please* – the new two-tiered pleasure pier was opened and was an instant success, with – *drumroll please* – 10,000 visitors in the first season. The 'working' pier and the 'fun' pier coexisted for many years side by side but, on 24 August, 1966, the *Embassy* paddle steamer was the last to use the new pier and the once-bustling seaside attraction was left to deteriorate for almost 30 years. If the Swanage Pier Trust hadn't stepped in in 1994 to restore the pier (raising over £1 million to do so), it'd likely have gone the same way as the old pier, which is now a wooden skeleton of its former self.

One of the very few wooden piers left in the UK, it's under constant threat from gribble worms that munch away at the wood beneath the waves. Thus, every 25 years or so many of the piles need replacing, and £200,000 needs to be raised each year to keep the pier open. The owner of the brass plaque stating, 'Strolling on a pier is bliss' would agree this is money well-spent.

Address Pier Approach, Swanage BH19 2AW, +44 (0)1929 425806,
www.swanagepiertrust.com, office@swanagepiertrust.com | Getting there By car, A350,
A35 and A351 to High Street in Swanage, then keep left; bus Breezer 30, Breezer 40 or
Breezer 50 to Swanage Bus Station | Hours See www.swanagepiertrust.com/opening-
and-parking as times vary seasonally | Tip The 1859 Pier Cafe & Bistro (named after the
year of construction of the original Swanage Pier) has three glass floor panels so you can
see the historic saltwater baths that once stood here in Marine Villas.

94__ Thomas Kirk Wright Boat

A real lifesaver

Dubbed the 'miracle of Dunkirk', Operation Dynamo (27 May to 4 June, 1940) saw more than 338,000 British, French and other Allied soldiers rescued from the beaches and harbour of Dunkirk in France, after being surrounded by the German army. Around 850 small vessels from all over the south of England, including speedboats, fishing boats, yachts, ferries, tugboats, pleasure boats and lifeboats, were called upon to help in this Dunkirk evacuation.

One such lifeboat was *Thomas Kirk Wright* (owned by the Royal National Lifeboat Institution – RNLI), which was one of the first lifeboats to reach the scene on 30 May. The boat's lack of propellers meant it could get right up to the beach. The 32-foot boat made three trips over four days, carrying hundreds of troops to safety. On the final trip, it came under machine-gun fire from German troops. No one was shot but the boat was severely damaged, with one of the engines burned out and a foot of water in the hull. Brave boat that it was, it returned to Poole, got patched up and resumed rescuing people for the RNLI, until 1962 when it was finally removed from service.

Thomas Kirk Wright was built in 1938 at a cost of £3,337, funded by a legacy from Mr Thomas H. Kirk Wright of Bournemouth. After 23 years of RNLI service (where it was launched 68 times) and 12 years as a private boat for Poole local and ex-lifeboat volunteer Paul Neate, it now lives in Poole Old Lifeboat Station on Fisherman's Dock. For 92 years, this was a working station but is now a small museum housing, among other things, the original waterproofs and life jackets worn by the men who travelled to Dunkirk. There's also a letter from the RNLI to Wright's niece, who attended the boat's naming ceremony on 7 June, 1939. Referring to the boat, the letter states that the RNLI has 'every confidence that she will prove adequate for any task she may have to perform.'

Address Poole Old Lifeboat Station, Fisherman's Dock, The Quay, BH15 1HA, +44 (0)1202 666046, www.poolelifeboats.org.uk/poole-old-lifeboat-museum-and-shop | Getting there Located at the eastern end of Poole Quay, not far from Baiter Park | Hours Apr–early Dec daily 10am–4pm (dependent on volunteer availability and/or weather) | Tip If you fund an RNLI lifeboat, it will be named after you, but it'll cost anywhere between £52,000 and £2.1 million! Instead, donate to the charity to get a name displayed on the side of one of their boats (search 'Launch a Memory' on www.rnli.org).

95 Totem Poles at Holton Lee

Making faces

When you arrive somewhere, it's nice to be greeted by a friendly face. At Livability Holton Lee, you may see the odd friendly face on one of these 19 totem poles, but it'll be stacked amidst an array of strange, sinister and downright fascinating visages. This art installation, called *Oak Tree Gathering*, was created by a group of people working with the organisation 15 Days in Clay. Originally set up in 2003 for adults with learning/additional needs, the project participants met for 15 days over 15 weeks – hence the name – to mould, create and bond. Their remarkable 'Tribe' exhibition was displayed in The Lighthouse arts centre during February to April in 2019. Next to the totem poles, mounted on the wall of the Old Farmhouse, is a quirky collection of bat boxes, also the handiwork of 15 Days in Clay. As yet, no bats have been tempted to roost in any of them; the three species of resident bat prefer to live in the roof of this building, with another colony in the rafters of the adjacent Spinal Injury Centre.

Livability is a charity that works with adults with special needs, mental health problems, learning disabilities, dementia and those recovering from addiction. It runs its Flourish programme out of Holton Lee, a 350-acre nature reserve, where those involved try their hand at horticulture, conservation, gardening and rural crafts. Much of what they grow (onions, courgettes, potatoes) and make (garden signs, bird feeders, jam) is for sale in The Green Cabin shop.

Holton Lee is open to everyone and encourages visitors to explore its trails, gardens, walking routes, reedbed boardwalk, bird hides, harbour views, and sculptures around the estate that showcase the work of disabled artists, such as *Stuck in a Rut* and *Freebird*. But if you don't feel like stretching your legs, you can always just sit and 'face-time' these kooky/spooky characters near the entrance.

Address Livability Holton Lee, 74 East Holton, Holton Heath BH16 6JN, +44 (0)1202 625562, www.holtonlee.org | **Getting there** By car, A350, A35, at the roundabout take the first exit onto A351, Holton Lee is on the left | **Hours** Open 24 hours | **Tip** The birdwatching here is incredible, but to enjoy it from the comfort of your own home, Google 'Holton Lee webcam' and follow the link through the Birds of Poole Harbour website.

96 Thunderbird House

An extravagant abode with cult status

Dubbed by locals as the 'Marmite House' because you either love it or hate it, Thunderbird sat on the market for a decade, before finally being sold in 2015 for £1.9 million – less than half the original £4-million asking price. Property magnate Eddie Mitchell used the fictional Tracy Island headquarters in the 1960s cult TV show *Thunderbirds* as inspiration, and included design features such as a curved building, blue glass windows and a wing-shaped copper roof to set his lavish, futuristic property apart. It's been said that he paid £900,000 for the land and spent between £1 million and £2 million constructing his vision.

While the Branksome Park one-of-a-kind home doesn't release jets or have a missile-launching pad, it's still pretty high-tech, with most electronics – from the heating to the lighting to the curtains – being operated from a single keypad. In keeping with the space-age theme, the stairwell has more than 1,000 fibre-optic, colour-changing lights and there's a kaleidoscope glass floor that has ever-changing hues. There are also five en-suite bedrooms, three extra bathrooms, a cinema, a 50-foot heated outdoor pool, a gym, a triple-car garage and a roomy 100-foot living area spanning the ground floor.

When it first went on the market in 2005, around 100 people queued up to take a look. Among those interested were a lord, a racing driver, a footballer and Oasis frontman Liam Gallagher. Alas, it didn't sell and so instead has been rented out over the years at £6,000 a month.

Just like the Thunderbirds' radio sign-off, many consider the luxury abode to be F.A.B., awarding it with a number of accolades, including Best Private Home in the 2006 National Home Builder Design Awards, and the Pride of Place Award in the same year, bestowed by Poole Council for the innovative design that made a positive contribution to the area. Thunderbirds are go!

Address 16 Western Avenue, Branksome Park BH13 7AN | Getting there Parkstone Road, Bournemouth Road, right onto North Lodge Road, right onto Canford Cliffs Road to Western Avenue. This is a private residence so can't be entered, but the house can be seen through the gates. | Tip An entrance to Branksome Chine beach is a few minutes' walk away. When you reach it, stroll through the chine to Branksome Beach Restaurant for a rest and some refreshment (www.branksomebeach.co.uk).

97_ Truly Scrumptious
Gimme some sugar

Pop quiz: Which wizard-esque film star has visited this retro sweet shop to stock up on treacle toffees? No idea? How about this one: Which retail guru bought an ice cream for her son here and commented on what a lovely shop it is? Answers: Sir Ian McKellen and Mary Portas.

Step inside this nostalgic sweet emporium, lined with over 220 jars of sweeties, and you'll be like a kid in a, er, candy store. Will your sweet tooth be drawn to one of the best-selling rhubarb and custards, sherbet lemons or bonbons (of which there are 10 different flavours, from lemon to raspberry, toffee to strawberry); or the cabinet containing chocolates with over 50 different fillings; or one of the 15 flavours of fudge made in the shop; or one of the seven varieties of Turkish delight; or perhaps a selection of your favourite penny sweets from your childhood – sherbet pips, foam shrimps or cherry lips, anyone?

Previously a stable for the horses belonging to the Antelope Hotel, the shop as it stands now has been in Poole Old Town for 17 years. A few additions have been made, like the bubble machine placed over the door that blasts out floaty orbs of enticement, inviting those young at heart to pop in for a yummy treat. Just follow the bubbles! As well as selling goodies over the counter, Truly Scrumptious also provides dentist-disapproved delights for corporate events, kids' parties and weddings. One such wedding was held at the nearby Scaplen's Court, and the bride and groom issued a ticket for each guest to use during the reception for a Lovingtons ice cream. You could say that when it came to keeping their guests happy, they had it licked.

With its huge array of sweet treats, Truly Scrumptious would definitely get the thumbs-up from king of candy Willy Wonka himself. And if Mary Portas finds it agreeable (does that woman know her shops!), it's got to be good.

Address 5 High Street, BH15 1AB, +44 (0)1202 674117, www.thepinksugarmouse.com | Getting there 12-minute walk from Poole Bus Station, 2-minute walk from Poole Quay | Hours Mon–Sat opens at 10am, Sun opens at 10.30am, seasonal closing times apply (check facebook.com/trulyscrumptiousdorsetltd) | Tip When you've finished indulging your inner child, let your adult self out to play at the Tin of Sardines gin bar next door (www.tinofsardinespoolequay.co.uk).

98_ Tyneham Ghost Village

The place that time forgot

Everyone likes getting mail… except when it's a letter from the War Office telling you to evacuate your home within a month. This is what happened to the 225 residents of Tyneham in November 1943, because their village and the surrounding area were needed for military training in the run-up to D-Day. Come 19 December, with very little Christmas cheer in the air, everyone was gone. Little did they know they would never return.

In 1952, the government bought the entire valley for £30,000. Today, the area is owned by the Ministry of Defence and military training still occurs but – after much campaigning (including a 1972 placard reading 'John Gould was born at Tyneham 60 years ago. He wants to go home') – it was decided that it would also be open to the public at specific times.

Dubbed in the press as 'the village that died for D-Day', Tyneham is like a time warp. Bylaws prevent the commercial development of the area, which is why you won't find a gift shop or cafe here. Wander around the now-roofless cottages, each with an information board depicting photos and facts about the previous dwellers. The names of some of the cottages, like Gardener's Cottage, Laundry Cottage and Shepherd's Cottage, give an indication of how villagers earned a living. The 1920 schoolroom has been recreated, with study books open on the desks, a nature table holding an array of shells, and an ominous-looking cane on Mrs Pritchard's desk.

The church has also had a facelift – look out for the villagers' family names on the frieze of tiles around the building. Before leaving her home, Evelyn Bond, who lived in the grand Tyneham House, pinned a poignant notice to the church door, reading: 'Please treat the church and houses with care. We have given up our homes… to help win the war… We will return one day and thank you for treating the village kindly.' If only she'd known…

Address East Lulworth, Wareham BH20 5DE | **Getting there** By car, A35, A351 towards Swanage. Just after Wareham turn right and follow signs to Creech/Kimmeridge, then Tyneham. The turning to Tyneham village is on the left. | **Hours** Due to military training, access is limited, but the area is open most weekends. For opening times, visit www.dorsetforyou.gov.uk/lulworth-range-walks | **Tip** It's about a one-mile walk to Worbarrow Bay, where the schoolchildren of Tyneham were often taken for picnics.

99 'Uncle Albert's' Grave
Laughing all the way from the bank

'This time next year we'll be millionaires,' 'Cushty', 'Mange tout'...
Just a few amusing phrases made famous by the classic British TV
programme *Only Fools and Horses*. You can add 'During the war...'
to the list, thanks to Del Boy and Rodney's Uncle Albert, who was
played by Buster Merryfield. Merryfield was a much-loved member
of the Verwood community (he lived on Manor Road), and when
he died in Poole Hospital of a brain tumour in 1999, aged 78, hundreds of people attended his funeral at St Michael and All Angels
Church, including co-stars David Jason and Nicholas Lyndhurst. He
is buried in Verwood Cemetery, alongside his wife, Iris. Nicknamed
'Buster' by his grandpa as he weighed nine pounds at birth, Merryfield's real name was Harry. Not many people knew this, however,
as 'Buster' refused to divulge it. The Captain Birdseye doppelgänger
came to professional acting late in life, at 57, having spent 40 years
as a NatWest bank manager.

Although Verwood never featured in *Only Fools and Horses*, other
locations around Poole did. Studland Beach posed as Benidorm in 'It
Never Rains' and sees Del Boy sunbathing in a pair of leopard-print
budgie smugglers in front of the dunes. Although it's supposed to
be Spain, there's a complete lack of high-rise hotels and you can see
the Truckline Ferry in the distance! Claysmore Boarding School in
Iwerne Minster (a village near Blandford) is in 'A Touch of Glass', an
episode that attracted more than 10 million viewers, and features the
comedy-gold moment when a chandelier crashes to the floor after
Grandad loosens the wrong bolt. What a plonker!

Only Fools and Horses has had many a classic moment – your
sides may still be recovering from when Del Boy fell through the
bar. If you visit Merryfield Close in Verwood, named after Buster,
try to recall as many as you can and have a little chuckle to yourself.
Lovely jubbly!

Address Verwood Cemetery, 166 Verwood Road, Verwood BH31 7FZ | **Getting there** By car, A35 and A338 to B3081. Drive through the cemetery gates and curve to the left. Park by the turning circle and walk to the first bench. The grave is directly in front of it, three rows back. | **Tip** In 1992, Merryfield dressed as Santa to feature in a TV advert for local caravan park Rockley Park (www.haven.com/parks/dorset/rockley-park). Check it out on YouTube for a giggle.

100__ W. E. Boone and Co Ltd

Sells everything but bubbles for spirit levels

The oldest shop in Poole and one of the oldest hardware stores in Britain, W. E. Boone and Co Ltd has been trading since 1820. Step inside and you'll not only be hit with the sight of higgledy-piggledy, floor-to-ceiling, wall-to-wall merchandise – everything from scissors to screwdrivers, Zimmer frame feet to tea bag squeezers, you'll also be hit with a sense of nostalgia and an extremely British 'Keep Calm and Carry On' vibe.

Priding itself on good, old-fashioned customer service (there is a tap under the counter so staff can demonstrate how to change a washer to head-scratching customers), W. E. Boone has become something of an institution on Poole High Street. It currently stands at number 91, but up until around 1895, it was number 77. At this time, the town planners decided to rotate the numbering system – instead of having number 1 start at the town boundary (near where the railway track is today) and go down to Poole Quay, it was agreed that the numbers would begin at the quay.

In 1886, the shop traded under the name Farmer & Co. It was from here that the revolver used to shoot Poole former mayor Alderman Horatio Hamilton outside The Guildhall (ch. 34) was purchased.

Such is the uniqueness of this traditional ironmonger that a 156-page book has been written about it: *Have You Got Four Candles?* by James Addison. Its title is inspired by the classic 1976 *The Two Ronnies* comedy sketch, which sees Ronnie Barker enter a hardware store similar to W. E. Boone and ask for 'fork handles', in response to which he is given 'four candles'. The sketch has featured highly on many 'funniest TV moment' lists and the original handwritten script was auctioned for £48,500 in 2007. It became so iconic for Ronnie B. and Ronnie C. that they both had four candles on display at their memorial services. 'It's goodnight from me. And it's goodnight from him.'

Address 91 High Street, BH15 1AW, +44 (0)1202 674010 | **Getting there** 10-minute walk from Poole Bus Station, 5-minute walk from Poole Quay | **Hours** Mon–Sat 8.30am–5pm | **Tip** Other old-school hardware stores in the area are C.J's Hardware (125–127 Bournemouth Road) and Blake's Domestic Stores (98 Sandbanks Road). Buy local or bye local.

101 Wareham Bears

Grizzlies playing dress-up

If you go down to the woods today… you'll see over 200 miniature bears arranged in all manner of different scenarios. Some will be playing rugby, some will be fishing, others will be at the stables, the more cultured will be at the theatre, the green-fingered will be gardening, and yet others will be perched atop a gypsy wagon.

These unusual yet enchanting bears live at Blue Pool, which dominates a 25-acre heath, woodland and gorse estate that was declared a Site of Special Scientific Interest (SSSI) in 1985. Despite being called 'Blue', the pool actually constantly varies in colour – a spectrum from green to turquoise – due to the very fine clay suspension in the water which diffracts light in different ways. You won't find the Wareham Bears nipping down for a sneaky dip, though – the pool isn't suitable for swimming for people, dogs or, indeed, miniature bears.

This sleuth of bears is the work of Mary Hildesley, who began collecting and dressing them in 1974, initially buying a few small bears from Harrods. When Harrods stopped stocking them, she tracked down the company that produced them and bought all of the six-inch bears they had – about 300 in total. Soon the characters started taking on a life of their own and Mary created stories of the bears in action, photographing them to make a scrapbook. She progressed to pastel drawings of the bears, which can now be seen on the Wareham Bears postcards and in the series of 12 books she wrote, including *Meet The Wareham Bears* and *The House of Bears*. She gave these original bears away to family and friends but later commissioned artist and sculptor John Honeychurch to recreate them. The collection initially only delighted Mary's grandchildren, but it soon grew and was opened to the public in 1981. Now, approximately 50,000 bear-loving – or perhaps just bear-curious – people visit the Wareham Bears each year.

Address Old Furzebrook Road, Wareham BH20 5AR, +44 (0)1929 551408, www.bluepooltearooms.co.uk, info@bluepooluk.com | **Getting there** By car, Blandford Road, A35, A351 to Furzebrook Road | **Hours** Easter–end of Oct, daily 10am–4.30pm | **Tip** Blue Pool also has a museum, which highlights the history of clay mining in the area and the interesting story of the local clay industry. There's a tearoom onsite, too.

102 Wareham Market Statue

The past set in stone

Birds and rabbits strung up, meat being cleavered, a dog licking a lamb, a sheep feeding its young, flowers being sold, a grandfather clock toppling over, a cello balancing precariously… There's rather a lot going on in this sculpture. But, then, there's been rather a lot going on in Wareham's markets over the past 700 years (and continues to be), which is what this 11-and-a-half-foot Portland stone statue represents.

It took local sculptor Jonathan Sells eight months to carve the showpiece, which was commissioned in 2003 by Ward Bullock, the then-owner of Cottees auction house (Cottees had previously managed the markets for 100 years). He had wanted to celebrate Wareham's markets in all their bustling, chaotic glory by displaying the sculpture outside Cottees. Most of the faces on the sculpture are of real people, including Bullock himself, moonlighting as the butcher. Sells injected some sardonic humour into the piece – there's a hand under the butcher's table (representing survival), scrabbling on the floor for scraps. Cottees' Wareham showroom closed and, in 2015, moved to its present site on Mannings Heath Road. The sculpture almost didn't make the move but, such was the public outcry at the news that it was planned to be auctioned off, that the new Cottees owner withdrew it from auction and placed it outside the current building, which is where it remains.

Sells has adorned other parts of town with his handiwork. Outside the Bournemouth International Centre (BIC) stands the jovial *Tregonwell and Creeke* sculpture, depicting two men greatly involved in the development of the area. Tregonwell holds a bucket and spade, and Creeke is sat on the loo! There's also the *Primordial* sculpture outside the Heritage Centre at Lulworth Cove, which shows dinosaurs and other creatures that would have lived on the Jurassic Coast 250 million years ago.

Address Cottees Auctions Limited, Mannings Heath Road, BH12 4NQ,
+44 (0)1202 723177, www.cottees.co.uk, info@cottees.co.uk | Getting there Bus 16 or
17 towards Bournemouth, or 14 towards Bournemouth Hospital, to Alderney Post Office.
The statue is round the back of Cottees, next to Cottees Cafe. | Tip You won't be able
to miss the 33-foot-long scrap-metal dinosaur outside the front of Cottees. She's called
Wanda, following a social-media competition asking people to name her.

103 — Wareham Town Pound
History on the hoof

BAA! NEIGH! MOO! CLUCK! OINK! You might have heard this farmyard chorus if you were anywhere near this small, enclosed square in the historic market town of Wareham during medieval times. The pound would have held stray or impounded farm animals until the owner paid a fine to the Lord of the Manor to release their beast. If the animals weren't claimed, they would be sold at the market to the highest bidder, with the money going to the pound keeper (*rubs his hands together in glee*). Most medieval villages and towns had a pound, often used as a temporary prison for petty criminals until the local authorities figured out what to do with them. The town stocks were placed there as a means of punishment or public humiliation. Now a Grade II listed building, if you look on the back wall of Wareham Town Pound, you can still see the rusty hook where the animals (and perhaps criminals) would have been tethered.

Over the years, this pound became overgrown and ignored, which is why a community art project was implemented to give it a new lease of life in 2011, funded by donations from the local community. Students from Purbeck School worked with local artist Maria Burns (who is also responsible for the sea-life mural at Pinecliff Gardens on Canford Cliffs clifftop) to create life-size, aluminium sculptures of animals that may once have been found in the pound, illustrated with collages, sketches and photos of Wareham.

There are other sites around Poole that recall the days of rogue, roaming animals being contained in animal pounds. These are marked by black, wooden signs that state: 'Site of the ancient pound… Formerly under the jurisdiction of the Lord of the Manor of Canford' on one side, and 'This was used for the impounding of straying cattle' on the other. Such signs can be found on Pound Lane opposite Tesco Express and by Halfords on Ringwood Road.

Address Pound Lane, Wareham BH20 4LQ | **Getting there** Enter Wareham along Worgret Road and park in Streche Road car park on the left, opposite the pound; Breezer buses 40 and 30, and First X54, to Wareham | **Tip** Climb the grass bank by the Streche Road car park and look towards Wareham. Through the chimneys, you'll be able to catch a glimpse of Corfe Castle in the distance.

104 Washington Coat of Arms

Where America earned its (stars and) stripes

Around 332.3 million people live in America. As they're singing the national anthem at a sporting event, or pledging allegiance to the flag at school, it's unlikely that even one of them is thinking about the tiny hamlet of Steeple in Dorset. Yet it's here where a special, historic connection to their country's first president, George Washington, lies. This coat of arms – seen in the main porch, above a doorway and on the ceiling of St Michael and All Angels Church – is the result of two families merging. In 1390, Edmund Lawrence married heiress Agnes de Wessington (an ancestor of George Washington). The crusader cross belonged to the Lawrence family, while the stars and stripes (whose 'proper' names are 'mullets and bars') belonged to the Washington family. While the Lawrences moved to Steeple in 1540, the Washingtons moved to Virginia in America. This 'mash-up' coat of arms is identical to the design engraved into George Washington's signet ring, and provided the inspiration for the American flag we know today.

To honour this association, the mayor of Washington D.C., Walter E. Washington, presented St Michael and All Angels Church with the city's flag in 1977. It is now hanging on the wall near the 1858 barrel organ. The letter the enthusiastic mayor wrote to the church's rector is framed and displayed, too. In it, he credits a 'Mr. George Honebon of Poole' with enlightening him on the church's relationship with the family of George Washington, and explains that he's waving Honebon off back to England with the letter and flag, 'thinking that your parish might appreciate having some token of our mutual heritage.' What a thoroughly decent chap, flying the flag for friendship between England and America. All together now: *The laaaand of the freeee, and the hoooome of the braaaave.*

Address St Michael and All Angels Church, Steeple, Wareham BH20 5NY, +44 (0)1929 480257, www.steeplechurch.co.uk | Getting there By car, A350, A35, A351, Grange Road and Grange Hill | Tip St Laurence Church in Affpuddle also has American connections, with the same coat of arms displayed there.

105_ Wellington Clock Tower

One man's trash is another man's treasure

The Wellington Clock Tower's name is a bit like a Wonderbra in that it promotes false advertising. You see, it has no Wellington and no clock. Originally constructed in 1854 as a memorial for the Duke of Wellington, the intention was to include a statue of him but, funded by the public, local businesses and railway companies, the money ran out and this part had to be omitted. Carts rattling past disturbed the delicate mechanism inside the original clock, and it kept such poor time that it was removed and not replaced.

The Wellington Clock Tower (or just 'Tower') now stands on Swanage seafront but began its life in the Big Smoke, at the Southwark end of London Bridge. It's one of the many structures from London brought here by Swanage local George Burt in the 19th century. Burt worked for a London building company and would transport Purbeck stone to the city to be used in the construction of buildings there. It was unsafe to sail home with an empty boat, so he'd load up his ships with ballast – such as the dismantled Wellington Clock Tower, taken down in 1860 as it had become an obstruction to the traffic on London Bridge – to weigh them down. Wander around Swanage (or 'old London by the sea') and you'll see many more London leftovers. The facade of the Town Hall was originally part of Mercers' Hall; the columns on Convent Mews are from London's Millbank Prison; many of the cast-iron bollards still bear the name of the London borough they had resided in; and the two Ionic columns in Prince Albert Gardens were also originally from London. In 1875, Burt built Purbeck House (now Purbeck House Hotel), festooning it with many a London remnant, such as an archway from Hyde Park, a gargoyle from Westminster Hall and a tiled floor from the Houses of Parliament. Well, waste not, want not.

Address Peveril Point Road, Swanage BH19 2BB | Getting there By car, A350, A35 and A351 to High Street in Swanage, then continue onto Peveril Point Road. Park in the car park on Broad Road, walk through the Peveril Point Boat Park and onto the beach for a better view. Bus Breezer 30, Breezer 40 or Breezer 50 to Swanage Bus Station. | Tip The front of Purbeck House Hotel is covered with granite chippings, recycled from waste material from the construction of the steps of the Albert Memorial in Hyde Park.

106_ Westfield House

Bloody hell

Jack the Ripper was the nickname given to the killer of five pros-
titutes in Whitechapel in London between August and November
1888. He was never caught and the identity of the man with a penchant for slitting women's throats and removing their internal organs
remains a mystery. One of the prime suspects, however, was Mon-
tague John Druitt, who grew up in Westfield House in Wimborne.
It was the largest house in town, with stables and servants' cottages
set in the grounds. It has since been converted into flats.

Inspector Macnaghten of the London Metropolitan Police
believed Druitt to be Jack the Ripper and wrote a memorandum
outlining why. In it, he explains that after Druitt was found dead
in the Thames on 31 December (a verdict of suicide was recorded),
the murders ceased. Druitt had gone missing shortly after the final
murder and his body had been in the water for a month or more.
Macnaghten also explains that Druitt's family believed him to be
the ripper, and that he was 'sexually insane' (whatever that means –
shudder). Druitt's father, William Druitt, was Wimborne's leading
surgeon and some think it was observing his father's work that led
to the anatomical knowledge of how to remove someone's innards.
After Druitt's suicide, no more murders with Jack the Ripper's modus
operandi occurred and the police considered the case closed.

Over the years, though, the list of suspects has increased dramat-
ically and there are now more than 100 theories as to his identity.
'Ripperology' has become a macabre fascination for many authors,
academics and have-a-go detectives.

Druitt is buried at Wimborne Minster, home also of the Druitt
Window, an impressive stained-glass window dedicated to the memory of Druitt's parents. Paid for by their children, it depicts biblical
references to healing the sick. If Druitt was Jack the Ripper, the irony
of this is palpable.

Address Westfield Close, Wimborne BH21 1JX | **Getting there** By car, A350, Broadstone Way, B3074, Wimborne Road and B3078 to Westfield Close | **Tip** Inspector Frederick George Abberline, well-known for his police work on the Jack the Ripper case, retired to 195 Holdenhurst Road, and there is a plaque there in his honour.

107__White Mill Bridge

A sign of conviction

Australia: land of over 10,000 sandy beaches, more sunshine days than you can shake a flip-flop at and, er, Harold Bishop. There are worse places to end up than Down Under and, in the 18th and 19th centuries, if you wanted a one-way ticket there, all you had to do was vandalise a bridge.

White Mill Bridge holds one of the many cast-iron plaques around Dorset that reads: 'Any person wilfully injuring any part of this county bridge will be guilty of felony and upon conviction liable to be transported for life by the court.' Between 1788 and 1868, around 162,000 convicts were exiled from Britain to penal colonies in Australia, mostly for petty crimes. Other local bridges with the same stern warning include those at Longham, Wool, Durweston, Charmouth, Wareham and Tuckton. If you were so inclined, you could've gone on a 'bridge-injuring' spree.

The 210-foot-long, 12-foot-wide White Mill Bridge is said to be the oldest bridge in Dorset. While the ironstone and limestone structure dates from the 16th century (with various repairs over the years), its foundations of timber pilings have been standing strong since the 12th century, and references were made in documents to 'a bridge on the River Stour adjacent to the White Mill' in 1175. White Mill, now a National Trust property, is an 18th-century disused corn mill. There were once eight mills on this stretch of river, but this is the only one that remains. The bridge has eight semicircular arches, the four in the middle being larger than the ones on either side. Just as it was in the past, it's still protected by law, now being a Grade I listed building and a scheduled ancient monument. If you're thinking of taking a sledgehammer to it however, hoping for a flight to Australia, you'll be disappointed. If you want to be transported to Oz, it's much easier – and less destructive – to tune in to *Neighbours*.

Address Mill Lane, Sturminster Marshall, Wimborne Minster BH21 4BX | Getting there By car, A350, right onto Station Road, at the roundabout continue straight to High Street, then Church Street, then Mill Lane | Tip The Tolpuddle Martyrs were a group of Dorset-ites famously sentenced to penal transportation to Australia. Discover their story at the Tolpuddle Martyrs Museum (www.tolpuddlemartyrs.org.uk).

108_ Wildlife Tiles

In their nature

As you're wrestling with the trolleys at the Alder Park Sainsbury's, take a moment to look at the tile panel next to them. You'll be met with an array of painted wildlife – frogs, snakes, lizards, birds, dragonflies, butterflies, insects – that take up residence on the nearby Talbot Heath and the surrounding Poole heathland.

Note particularly the ladybird spider on the far left of the mural. These dotty critters are one of the most endangered species of spider in the UK. They were thought to be extinct for more than 70 years, but in 1980, a few were discovered crawling about in Dorset. Conservation work has subsequently seen their population increase to around 1,000.

At the opposite end of the mural is a Dartford warbler, standing guard over its nest of eggs. This rare bird saw its Dorset population decrease drastically with the bitter winters of the early 1960s, then again with the heath fires of 1976, but has since gradually recovered. Sand lizards and smooth snakes also make an appearance on these tiles. Both are very rare outside of Dorset, with the county supporting 80 per cent of the national population of sand lizards, and 90 per cent of the smooth snake (Britain's rarest reptile).

On the first Monday of every month, Walking for Health hosts the Talbot Heath Educational Walk. The group meets by this mural, then is taken to Talbot Heath for a wander. You'll criss-cross over Bourne Stream several times, walk past Highmoor Farm (which was set up by the Talbot sisters in the 19th century to provide food for Poole residents, but is now under threat from developers), witness a small waterfall flowing from what locals call 'the hidden lake' (which, obviously, you won't see) and, if you time it right, watch dragonflies, damselflies and butterflies dancing above the stream, while trout wiggle their fins below the waterline. It's quite a walk on the wild(life) side.

CALLUNA VULGARIS · ERICA TETRALIX · SALIX CINEREA · TYPHA LATIFOLIA

libellula vulva · aeshna mixta · STONECHAT · saxicola torqua

SMOOTHSNAKE · COMMON LIZARD · ceriagrion tenellum · thyric

SILVER STUDDED BLUE · COMMON FROG · SAND ASP

Address Sainsbury's, Alder Park, 4 Alder Road, BH12 4BA, www.walkingforhealth.org.uk | **Getting there** By car, Parkstone Road, Ashley Road to Alder Road; bus 17 towards Bournemouth to Sainsbury's | **Tip** The nearby Alder Hills Nature Reserve is also home to the species on the mural. The lake in the centre was developed from a flooded clay pit abandoned in 1948. (The entrance to the reserve is at the end of Sharp Road.)

109__ Wimborne Chained Library

A bibliophile's paradise

There's little risk of an overdue fine at this library in Wimborne Minster, as many of the books have never ventured farther than the length of a chain. The third-largest chained library in the UK, it was founded in 1686 by Reverend William Stone, and originally contained around 90 religious texts that he had donated in a bid to keep them safe. He'd seen books like his burned by the authorities and didn't want his to suffer the same fate. It wasn't until 1695, when a further collection of books was donated by Roger Gillingham, that chains were added, at his insistence, and it became one of the earliest public libraries in the country. Books are abundant now, but back then, they were so rare that theft was a real concern.

The oldest book in the library is the *Regimen Animarum*, dated 1343, with only two others in existence. Vegans may be horrified to learn that it's written on 80 calf skins, known as vellum. It's been estimated that it took almost a year to hand write, using a quill. If a scribe made a mistake, he would use a razor to slice it away and then write over it. An old-school Tipp-Ex, if you will. This may be why we say 'eraser', as the Latin *erasus* meant 'scraped off'. *Regimen Animarum* translates as 'The Guiding of Souls', with the book containing a list of spiritual dangers and how to avoid them. Could this be the first ever self-help book?

Among the other 380 books (of which 150 are chained), is *Walton's Polyglot Bible*, the only Bible to be printed in nine languages. The collection of books has been described as a 'musty divinity' and, although many of them are religious, other subject matters range from politics to gardening, winemaking to etiquette. On the latter subject, the 1672 *The Gentleman's Companion* by William Ramsay strongly recommends that men don't marry, but instead spend their time inventing ships and aircraft.

Address Wimborne Minster, High Street, Wimborne BH21 1EB, +44 (0)1202 884753, www.wimborneminster.org.uk, parishoffice@wimborneminster.org.uk | Getting there By car, A350, A349 and B3073; bus 3 or 4 towards Wimborne Minster, to The Square | Hours Apr–end of Oct Mon 2–4pm, Tue–Fri 10.30am–12.30pm & 2–4pm, 1st Sat of month 10.30am–12.30pm | Tip Michael Portillo featured Wimborne's Chained Library in the 'Brockenhurst to Poole' episode of his *Great British Railway Journeys* TV series.

110_ Wimborne Model Town

Honey, I shrunk the town

Wimborne Model Town is larger than life. Only… smaller. It is a one-tenth scale model of the market town of Wimborne exactly as it was in the 1950s. It has over 100 miniature shops, cafes, pubs, banks and other buildings such as public toilets, which flush, and a phone box, which rings. It also has a mini replica river system of the River Allen that runs through Wimborne. Not forgetting the grand (yet diddy) Wimborne Minster, made of 20 tonnes of concrete and as true to the real one just up the road as can be. Its stained-glass windows were created via 3D printing based on digital photos of the actual minster, and the hourly bell dong is a recording from the real deal. The Quarter Jack (ch. 74), a tiny Napoleonic soldier, lives high on the minster and bangs his bells every 15 minutes, two minutes after the actual one so he can be heard. Peer inside the minster and you'll see a wedding scene, complete with nervous-looking groom, dodgy bridesmaids' dresses and a troop of Brownies. At 11am and 2pm every day, Mendelssohn's 'Wedding March' bursts into life and a genuine recording from the minster is played, with the vicar addressing his congregation – 'Dearly beloved, we are gathered here today…'.

This teeny town of yesteryear was opened in 1951, and enjoyed two decades of success – by 1959, 80,000 people had visited. In 1983, however, it was closed due to a decline in visitors. Thankfully, it was moved, rebuilt and re-established as a charity run by volunteers in 1991. National treasure Roy Castle reopened it. Since then, it's gone from strength to strength, with many elements being added, including the working model railway, sensory garden, crazy-golf course, 1950s school set-up, tea room, and dolls' house collection donated by local enthusiast Beryl Dade. The whole place is a diminutive delight and, what it lacks in size, it makes up for in nostalgic charm.

Address King Street, Wimborne Minster BH21 1DY, +44 (0)1202 881924, www.wimborne-modeltown.com, info@wimborne-modeltown.com | **Getting there** By car, A350, A349 and B3073; bus 4, 13 or 6 towards Wimborne Minster, to The Square | **Hours** Late Mar–early Nov (check website for exact dates), daily 10am–5pm | **Tip** For another tiny treat, the Corfe Castle Model Village is a one-twentieth scale model of the castle and village as it was in 1646 (www.corfecastlemodelvillage.co.uk).

111 Winspit Quarry

Exterminate any feelings of blah

'Oh look, rocks!' exclaimed The Doctor as the door of his TARDIS slid open to reveal… rocks. These rocks were posing as part of the planet Skaro but, in reality, belonged to Winspit Quarry, and appeared in the 1979 episode of *Doctor Who*, 'Destiny of the Daleks'. In 1967, 'The Underwater Menace' episode was also filmed at this location, which passed itself off as a deserted volcanic island. Disney's 2012 sci-fi epic, *John Carter*, also got in on the rocky action, using Winspit as its Orkney Dig.

Besides being a sci-fi location scout's dream, this abandoned quarry is also a rock climber's paradise, with nearly 200 different climbing routes. Once climbers reach the top of the cliff, they can take in the beautiful view of the rugged coastline, plus see people picnicking on and swimming off the rocks below.

Up until 1940, Winspit was used as a stone quarry, providing building materials for many buildings in London. (In the 18th century, there were more than 200 quarries in Swanage, Worth Matravers and Langton Matravers.) During World War II, Winspit became a naval and air base, after which the privately owned caves were opened to the public. The remains of the old quarry buildings and houses are still there today.

In September 2010, Winspit became part of the Inside Out Dorset Festival, which promises 'extraordinary events in extraordinary places'. Extraordinary was right! The atmospheric 'Rock Charmer' event was held after dusk and combined the music of Finnish accordionist Kimmo Pohjonen with the animations of Dorset company The Paper Cinema. Pohjonen stood on a rock and 'bellowed' out his music, while images such as scrap-metal dinosaurs, fossils and shipwrecks were projected onto the cave walls. The audience watched, mesmerised… some perhaps even thinking, like a certain Time Lord, that they had been transported to a different planet.

Address Worth Matravers, Swanage BH19 3LY | Getting there By car, A350, A35, A351 and B3069 to Worth Matravers. Park at the car park near the Square & Compass pub, walk down the hill and follow the sign to Winspit (about a one-mile walk) | Tip Nearby Winspit Beach, Lulworth Cove and the caves at Dancing Ledge have all featured in *Doctor Who* episodes.

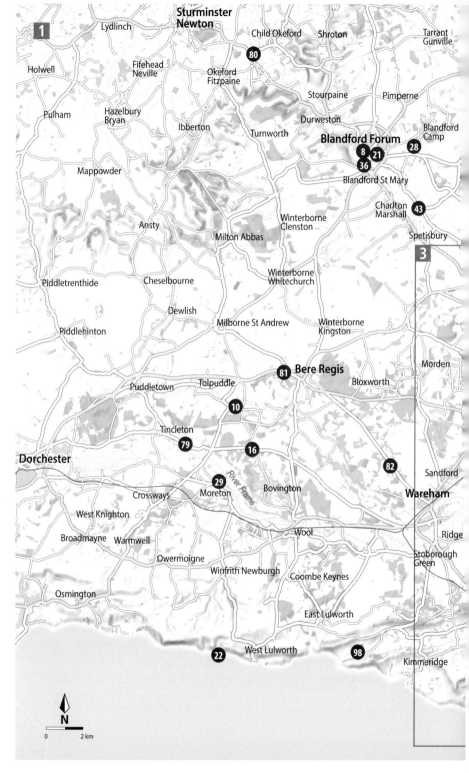

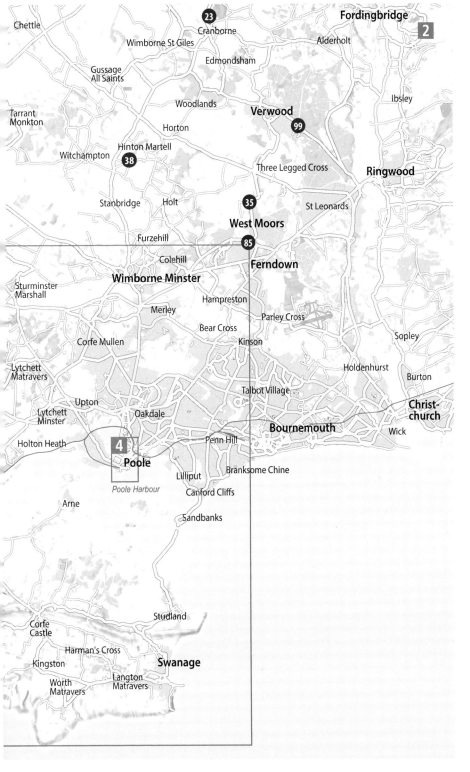

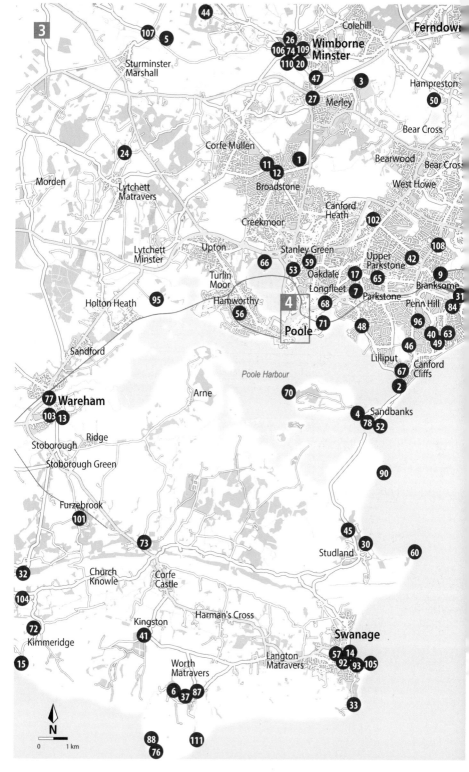

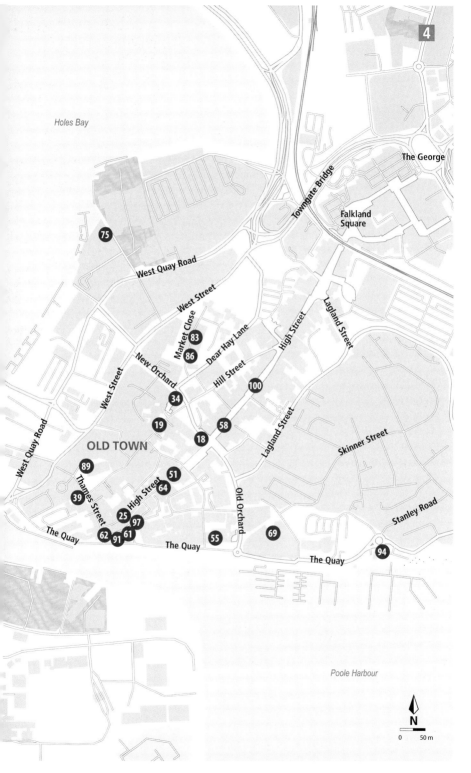

Maurizio Francesconi,
Alessandro Martini
111 Places in Turin
That You Shouldn't Miss
ISBN 978-3-7408-0414-5

Laszlo Trankovits
111 Places in Jerusalem
That You Shouldn't Miss
ISBN 978-3-7408-0320-9

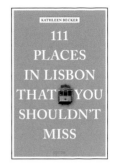

Kathleen Becker
111 Places in Lisbon
That You Shouldn't Miss
ISBN 978-3-7408-0383-4

Alexia Amvrazi,
Diana Farr Louis, Diane Shugart,
Yannis Varouhakis
111 Places in Athens
That You Shouldn't Miss
ISBN 978-3-7408-0377-3

Alexandra Loske
111 Places in Brighton and
Lewes That You Shouldn't Miss
ISBN 978-3-7408-0255-4

Fabrizio Ardito
111 Places in Malta
That You Shouldn't Miss
ISBN 978-3-7408-0261-5

Tom Shields, Gillian Tait
111 Places in Glasgow
That You Shouldn't Miss
ISBN 978-3-7408-0256-1

Andrea Livnat,
Angelika Baumgartner
111 Places in Tel Aviv
That You Shouldn't Miss
ISBN 978-3-7408-0263-9

Kay Walter, Rüdiger Liedtke
111 Places in Brussels
That You Shouldn't Miss
ISBN 978-3-7408-0259-2

Thomas Fuchs
111 Places in Amsterdam
That You Shouldn't Miss
ISBN 978-3-7408-0023-9

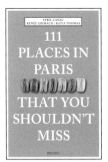

Sybil Canac, Renée Grimaud,
Katia Thomas
111 Places in Paris
That You Shouldn't Miss
ISBN 978-3-7408-0159-5

Matěj Černý, Marie Peřinová
111 Places in Prague
That You Shouldn't Miss
ISBN 978-3-7408-0144-1

Gillian Tait
111 Places in Edinburgh
That You Shouldn't Miss
ISBN 978-3-95451-883-8

Rosalind Horton,
Sally Simmons, Guy Snape
111 Places in Cambridge
That You Shouldn't Miss
ISBN 978-3-7408-0147-2

Justin Postlethwaite
111 Places in Bath
That You Shouldn't Miss
ISBN 978-3-7408-0146-5

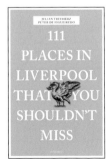

Julian Treuherz,
Peter de Figueiredo
111 Places in Liverpool
That You Shouldn't Miss
ISBN 978-3-95451-769-5

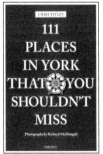

Chris Titley
111 Places in York
That You Shouldn't Miss
ISBN 978-3-95451-768-8

Frank McNally
111 Places in Dublin
That You Shouldn't Miss
ISBN 978-3-95451-649-0

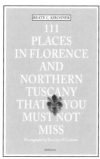

Beate C. Kirchner
**111 Places in Florence
and Northern Tuscany
That You Must Not Miss**
ISBN 978-3-95451-613-1

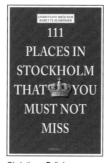

Christiane Bröcker,
Babette Schröder
**111 Places in Stockholm
That You Must Not Miss**
ISBN 978-3-95451-459-5

Marcus X. Schmid
**111 Places in Istanbul
That You Must Not Miss**
ISBN 978-3-95451-423-6

Annett Klingner
**111 Places in Rome
That You Must Not Miss**
ISBN 978-3-95451-469-4

Dirk Engelhardt
**111 Places in Barcelona
That You Must Not Miss**
ISBN 978-3-95451-353-6

John Sykes, Birgit Weber
**111 Places in London
That You Shouldn't Miss**
ISBN 978-3-95451-346-8

Peter Eickhoff
**111 Places in Vienna
That You Shouldn't Miss**
ISBN 978-3-95451-206-5

Lucia Jay von Seldeneck,
Carolin Huder
**111 Places in Berlin
That You Shouldn't Miss**
ISBN 978-3-7408-0589-0

Jo-Anne Elikann
**111 Places in New York
That You Must Not Miss**
ISBN 978-3-95451-052-8

Huge thanks to Jackie Broadhead, Pat Eggelton, Sophie Wright, Amanda Broom, Jez Martin, Steve Wallis and Viv Robertson for all your help and suggestions. Thanks also to my photographer, Oli Smith, and his super-duper assistant (and wife), Bec – the photos are beautiful. Mum, Dad, Ben, Josh and Toby: you also deserve high-fives and hugs for helping me to complete this book. Thank you for being top-notch research assistants, drive-arounders (sorry about the wild goose chases) and my biggest cheerleaders.

K. B.

Firstly, thank you to Katherine Bebo for giving me the chance to work with her on this book. It's really been an enjoyable collaboration where hopefully I've succeeded in adding some colour to her fantastic writing. Thanks also to everyone I visited for being so accommodating and welcoming me so warmly. Their help was much appreciated and crucial in order for me to capture any successful images. Finally a massive thank you to my wife Bec for choreographing everything: where I needed to go, when, who to meet and what to shoot. Without your liaising and organisational skills it would simply have been an impossible task for me to achieve.

O. S.

Katherine Bebo is a professional freelance writer and editor. Her career has taken her to London, Dubai and Denver in the USA… but now she's back home where her heart is: Poole (where she lives with her husband and two children). She has had a handful of books published – on topics ranging from films to fitness, cocktails to outer space – plus many features for well-known publications and websites.

Oliver Smith is a commercial photographer with more than 15 years' experience shooting properties, people and places all across the South of England. Following an extensive background in art and design, he gained his BA (hons) degree in photography in 2002 and ran a photographic laboratory for two years, before going freelance as Oliver Smith Photography. He lives with his wife and two children in Poole, where he continues to work amongst the high-end interiors and architectural market. His work has featured in a wide range of regional magazines, as well as national newspapers.